# The Search for an
# Abortionist

# The Search for an Abortionist

NANCY HOWELL LEE

THE UNIVERSITY
OF CHICAGO PRESS

**CHICAGO & LONDON**

*International Standard Book Number 0–226–47001–6*
*Library of Congress Catalog Card Number: 74–75135*
THE UNIVERSITY OF CHICAGO PRESS, CHICAGO 60637
The University of Chicago Press, Ltd., London
© 1969 by The University of Chicago
Published 1969
Second Impression 1972

Printed in the United States of America

# Contents

# Tables

## Figures

# *Preface*

The research on which this book is based was carried out between June 1965 and June 1967 in the Department of Social Relations, Harvard University. The original report on this research was submitted to the Department of Social Relations as a Ph.D. dissertation entitled "Acquaintance Networks in the Social Structure of Abortion." The research was supported by a Public Health Service Fellowship (5-F1-MH-24, 971-03 BHW) from the National Institute of Mental Health.

My primary acknowledgment is to the women who contributed to this study, especially to the twenty-five women who volunteered for personal interviews. I am sincerely and warmly grateful to the women who shared their personal experiences and feelings with me. Some of these women have thought long and clearly about the moral and psychological issues involved in abortion. A number of my ideas about these issues were suggested or clarified in the course of these interviews. I regret being unable to give personal credit to my informants for the intellectual contribution, as well as the informational contribution, that they made.

A large number of persons were involved in the study by helping or attempting to help me make contact with potential volunteer informants. Some of these people cannot be named, or have asked not to be named. It is a pleasure to have this opportunity to acknowledge the help of at least the following: Dr. Clarence Davis, of the Yale-New Haven Medical Center; Dr. William K. Rashbaum, New York; Dr. Aguiles Sobrero and the staff of the Margaret Sanger Research Bureau of New York; Mrs. Henry Wise and Mrs. Marie Reiser of Planned Parenthood of Rhode Island, in Providence; and especially Patricia Maginnis and Rowena Gurner of the Society for Humane Abortion in San Francisco. The help of all those who approached potential volunteers in the interest of this research is greatly appreciated.

A number of persons read earlier drafts of the research plans and preliminary results and made useful comments. I would like to thank Diana Russell Ekman, Michael Schwartz, Joel Levine, and Dr. Stanley Milgram of the Department of Social Relations; Drs. William Schmidt and James Teele of the Department of Maternal and Child Health of the Harvard School of Public Health; Dr. Steven Polgar, Research Director of Planned Parenthood-World Population; Dr. Charles Westoff of Princeton University; Drs. Everett C. Hughes and Robert S. Weiss of Brandeis University; and Dr. Charles Tilly of the University of Toronto. For contributions to my education in demography, and for helpful comments on an extensive preliminary paper on the exposure to risk of unwanted pregnancy, I would like to thank Dr. David Heer of Harvard University, Dr. Robert G. Potter, Jr., of Brown University, Dr. Mindel C. Sheps of Columbia University, and Dr. Christopher Tietze of the National Committee on Maternal Health, Inc.

Dr. George Goethals, of the Department of Social Relations, Harvard University, represented the departmental Committee on Research Responsibility by supervising the data collection to insure maximum protection of the informants from any unnecessary emotional stress in the course of the interviews. He listened to some of the tape-recorded interviews, without knowing the identity of the informants, and made many extremely interesting and useful suggestions about the interviews. Dr. A. J. Sobrero, Medical Director of the Margaret Sanger Research Bureau in New York, made a number of useful suggestions on the order, form, and content of the questions used in the questionnaire form.

Harrison C. White may have been surprised to find that his influence stimulated a study of induced abortion, yet I must give him full credit for providing the mental tools which made it possible for me to conceptualize the transmission of information about illegal activities as a problem in social structure. Professor White also provided practical help with this work, through informal and seminar discussions, by his reactions to a number of drafts of the ideas presented here, and by his concrete suggestions about the presentation of some of the data on communication networks. Any errors and obscurities which remain are my own fault.

The revision of the manuscript from a dissertation to book form was carried on primarily at the Dobe field-work station in the Kalahari desert of Botswana, concurrent with research on the demography of !Kung Bushmen. The difficulties of field conditions have made it impossible to revise the form of some of the presentations of data which might usefully have been simplified, and impossible to expand the present research to include the approximately one hundred questionnaires received after April 1967. I am particularly grateful to my friends Robert and Rebecca Thomas who invited me to share the comfort and convenience of the District Commissioner's residence in Maun, Botswana for three weeks while the bulk of the revision was being done. In addition, Mrs. Rebecca Thomas helped with the typing and editing of the revised version.

Finally, I would like to thank my husband, Richard Lee, for his consistent help.

*The Search for an Abortionist*

# 1

## The Social Structure of Abortion in America

Somehow, in the mysterious way that issues appear and disappear from the public agenda, abortion has arrived on the scene as a lively and current topic of debate. Only a few years ago, serious discussions of abortion were met with indifference or disbelief, and investigators despaired of finding a rational response from the public.[1] Today, it is widely acknowledged that abortion is one of the most common forms of illegal activity practiced in the United States, and revisions of the laws concerning abortion have been passed or are under consideration in many parts of the country. The explanation of why a subject is taboo at one time and au courant soon after is not obvious, and is, to a sociologist, as interesting a question as the practice of abortion itself.

Without attempting to explain the rapid change in interest and

[1] Alan Guttmacher refers to "the make-believe world of the non-existence of criminal abortion" in his Introduction to Bates and Zawadzki, *Criminal Abortion* (Springfield, Ill.: Thomas, 1964) and in 1966 Lawrence Lader started his book, *Abortion*, by saying "Abortion is the dread secret of our society" (Indianapolis: Bobbs Merrill Co., 1966).

3

opinion, we can note that it is related to a worldwide trend toward liberalization of the laws controlling access to medical abortions which is accompanying the great increases in population all over the world. Japan and most of the socialist countries have made it national policy to provide legal medical abortions upon the request of patients.[2] The Scandinavian countries and, since 1967, the United Kingdom make abortion available to women on an individual basis under a range of social, economic, and medical situations. In the United States, where abortion primarily comes under the jurisdiction of the states, the laws currently permit only medical factors to be taken into account in determining whether legal abortion shall be permitted, although the mental health clause of the laws of some states is used as an elastic provision to include some cases which primarily involve social factors.[3]

At the same time that interest in changing the laws has been developing, there has been a revolution in contraceptive technology. "The pill" was first approved for prescription use in the United States in June 1960. By 1967, an estimated five million American women were taking the pills every month.[4] The widespread acceptance of the pill, and the essentially zero rate of accidental conceptions associated with its use, suggests hope that the present rate of accidental conception, which amounts to several million per year,[5] can be drastically reduced and that the vast majority of unwanted pregnancies can be avoided before they occur.

The third factor involved in the increased interest in abortion is the promise of new pharmacological techniques of abortion. There

[2]See Christopher Tietze, "Some Facts about Legal Abortion," in Roy O. Greep, *Human Fertility and Population Problems* (Cambridge: Schenkman Publishing Co., 1963); and Andras Klinger, "Abortion Programs," in *Family Planning and Population Programs,* ed. Berelson *et al.* (Chicago: University of Chicago Press, 1965), pp. 465-76.

[3]The state laws of the United States and the relevant federal statutes are discussed in Lader, *Abortion.*

[4]Norman B. Ryder and Charles Westoff, "The National Fertility Study," presented to the Notre Dame Conference on Population, December 1966.

[5]This figure is intended as a very rough approximation, based on the estimate of one million induced abortions per year and the known high incidence of contraceptive failures among women who do not resort to abortion. See Charles Westoff *et al., Family Growth in Metropolitan America* (Princeton: Princeton University Press, 1961); and Robert G. Potter, Jr., "Some Relationships between Short Range and Long Range Risks of Unwanted Pregnancy," *Milbank Memorial Fund Quarterly* 38 (July 1960): 255-63.

have been numerous hints that a "morning-after" pill or a "once-a-month" pill will be available in the near future. Such a drug would eliminate the need for most operative abortions, legal or illegal.

Safe abortifacients, liberalization of abortion laws, and near-perfect contraceptive techniques may change the form of the abortion problem in the future, but they are utterly irrelevant to the experiences of the many women who have been seeking and finding abortions in the past and at the present time.

Of these women, we know very little. An accurate picture of the composition of the population of women who have abortions cannot be expected while abortion remains illegal and while people are understandably reluctant to answer questions which may place them in jeopardy. In the absence of accurate information based on random samples, a certain amount can be inferred from facts that are well established, or at least estimated on the basis of partial data. The size of the population of women who obtain deliberate abortions, for instance, is estimated as on the order of one million per year, although the true number may be as low as two hundred thousand or as high as two million.[6] Approximately ten thousand of these women succeed in having their abortions performed legally in a hospital;[7] the rest go to illegal practitioners in the United States or leave the country to seek abortion where it is more readily available. Most of the women who leave the country to have an abortion go to Canada, Mexico, or Puerto Rico, where the laws are similar to those of the United States, rather than travel to more distant countries where abortion is legal. It is known that many, perhaps most, abortions obtained in America are performed by physicians, many of whom continue to maintain a regular practice with abortion only a profitable sideline.[8] To say that most abortions are done by doctors is not to say that most doctors do abortions. It is clear that most physicians

[6]The first serious estimates of the incidence of abortion in America were made by Frederick J. Taussig, *Abortion, Spontaneous and Induced: Medical and Social Aspects* (St. Louis: C. V. Mosby Co., 1936). For more recent assessments of the probable incidence, see Christopher Tietze, "Introduction to the Statistics of Abortion," in *Pregnancy Wastage*, ed. E. T. Engle (Springfield: Thomas, 1953); and the "Statistical Appendix" to Mary S. Calderone, ed., *Abortion in the United States* (New York: Harper and Bros. and Paul H. Hoeber, 1958).

[7]See Tietze, "Some Facts about Legal Abortion."

[8]Paul H. Gebhard *et al.*, *Pregnancy, Birth and Abortion* (New York: Harper and Bros. and Paul H. Hoeber, 1958).

will not perform abortions outside a hospital, and do not offer any help to women who come to them in the hope of getting an abortion.[9] Some abortions are performed by abortionists who are not physicians. Many of these are older women trained as nurses or midwives, who perform abortions in their own homes or in their patients' homes.[10] Some abortionists are prosecuted by the law and sent to jail: most of these are arrested as a result of botched abortions which require the hospitalization of the patient.[11]

Of the women who get abortions, it is clear that not all, by any means, are unmarried women escaping illegitimacy. Studies of some groups, like the Kinsey group and various birth-control clinic populations, suggest that while the abortion rate is higher for unmarried women, married women, especially those who have had all the children they choose to have, probably obtain the majority of all abortions.[12] Estimates of the proportion of married women among abortion seekers vary from 40 to 90 percent.[13] Nor is abortion exclusively or even primarily an activity of one social class or another. Substantial numbers of both rich and poor women are known to obtain abortions.

The fact is that many people in the society manage to arrange an illegal abortion when they wish it, including vast numbers who are ordinarily law-abiding and perfectly respectable. This offers a somewhat startling perspective on our sometimes naive notions of how a complex society operates and how people operate within a complex society. The task of arranging an abortion is not a simple one. Whether or not the abortion seekers are aware of it, there is an effective time limit operating on the search for an abortionist. Most abortionists refuse to accept cases in which the pregnancy is advanced beyond the twelfth week, when induced abortions become more difficult and dangerous to perform. Since the pregnancy shows no signs before two weeks, and is rarely confirmed before five or six weeks, those seeking abortion usually have less than six weeks in which to

[9]Alan F. Guttmacher, "Therapeutic Abortion: Doctor's Dilemma," *Journal of Mt. Sinai Hospital*, vol. 21 (1954).

[10]Jerome E. Bates and Edward S. Zawadzki, *Criminal Abortion* (Springfield: Thomas, 1964).

[11]*Ibid.*

[12]See Gebhard *et al.*, *Pregnancy, Birth and Abortion*; and Endre K. Brunner and L. Newton, "Abortion in Relation to Viable Births in 10,609 Pregnancies," *American Journal of Obstetrics and Gynecology* 38 (1939) : 82-90.

[13]See Calderone, *Abortion in the United States.*

make a decision, locate an abortionist, raise whatever money is necessary, and have the abortion carried out.

This is a tight schedule of events—events which are complicated, difficult, and time-consuming. It is surprising, on one level, that such a large number of people are willing to undertake the risks of an illegal abortion rather than carry out the pregnancy. It is even more surprising, when one thinks about it, that hundreds of thousands of times each year people manage this complicated procedure, in the absence of institutional facilities to help them. One would think that the sheer level of activity generated by so many people carrying out such a demanding task would make abortion a highly visible activity in the society. Yet outside certain small circles, abortion is carried on almost invisibly. Many people know of a few cases among their friends and acquaintances; most physicians know of a larger number; and a few cases come to wide public attention when the patient dies or is taken to a hospital seriously ill. But still it is true to say that a very small amount of public notice is generated by what must be a great deal of activity.

Part of the explanation for the invisibility of abortion is that the participants, both patients and abortionists, are trying to keep it quiet to avoid confrontation with the law. Even the best intentions to keep it secret would not be successful, however, if it were not also true that the provision of illegal abortions is extremely decentralized. Each case is handled in an ad hoc way, working through the personal connections that individuals happen to have established before the need for abortion arose. Some of those who obtain abortions do not need to search for an abortionist, either because they find that they can have a legal hospital abortion, because they use self-induced techniques to perform it themselves, or because they happen to have access to a practicing abortionist. The vast majority of women, however, have to locate a specialist in abortion, an illegal practitioner who is willing to take the risks of breaking the law. These illegal practitioners, of course, cannot advertise their practice or make it freely available to their potential customers for fear of attracting the attention of law-enforcement agencies. Some abortionists are extremely surreptitious, operating from transient locations like hotel rooms and concealing their identity, even from their customers, by false names and even masks, while others remain in the same location for years and depend upon the loyalty and discretion of their customers to protect them from the law. In any case, there are no publicly

available channels like the yellow pages of the telephone directory which permit potential customers to locate abortionists. In order to find an abortionist, most people seem to ask their friends and acquaintances for leads, people who may not have information about abortionists but who do have the kind of relationship to those seeking abortion that motivates them to try to help and to keep quiet about it. To have an abortion, it is not necessary, initially, to know of an abortionist. Instead, one need only search through one's own acquaintances to find a person who has had some experience with abortion in the past. If there are no such persons among one's acquaintances, it is very likely that there will be among the acquaintances of those acquaintances. In this way, the individual asks for help from persons known to him or at least comes with an introduction from someone they both know. The activity is relatively invisible because the searches can be conducted through the channels of private conversations, telephone calls, and personal letters. The search, starting from ordinarily law-abiding citizens, can reach through a number of intermediary steps to an illegal practitioner without ever requiring the search to come into the public domain and involve a confrontation of strangers agreeing on an illegal activity.

This procedure depends upon a great deal of cooperation and participation by the persons who form the links between the couple who want to terminate the unwanted pregnancy and the abortionist. It must involve millions of Americans each year, both in direct participation in seeking abortion and in supplying information to those who are seeking. While there is no central organization or coordination, the association of those who perform abortions, the intermediary people who hold information on how to locate them, and those who seek abortions for themselves makes up an obscure form of social organization which is quite different from what we usually think of as social organization.

One tends to think of social structure as the ways in which large numbers of people are related to one another through social units to which they belong. One thinks of individuals belonging to families, families clustered into communities, communities into states, and states into a nation, for example. Or we think of individuals as related to others through their occupational roles, and groups of workers related to others through business organizations, through labor unions, or through markets. Consideration of the social structure of an activity like abortion requires the use of the concept of informal as well as formal types of social structure.

Social structure also includes the connections between persons which exist apart from organizations and institutions. The most general form of the question of informal social structure consists of the study of how individuals are related through their personal friends and acquaintances—what Simmel called overlapping social circles and what are now called acquaintance networks.[14] In recent years it has come to be called "the small world problem," from the cliché uttered when two complete strangers discover that they both know a third person.[15] Each person in a large society knows a certain number of others, which may be a very small proportion of the total number in the society. Each of those persons, in turn, knows a similar number of others, many of whom will not overlap with those known by the first person or others in the group known by the first person. Counting all one's acquaintances and all the acquaintances of one's acquaintances takes one to a large number. Carrying out the process a few more steps may include the majority of the people who live in the United States. It is possible, therefore, to describe the informal social structure of a large population by the length and complexity of the pathways formed by personal acquaintance among the members of the population.

The informal aspect of the social structure of abortion, similarly, consists of the connections between individuals who hold information about how abortions are arranged that has been used or could be used to provide contact between persons seeking abortion and abortionists. In order to clarify the concept of an information network and to begin to think in concrete terms of what the informal social structure of abortion must be like, even in the absence of empirical evidence, let us consider a hypothetical data collection and analysis that would shed light on the subject.

Imagine that every adult in the United States has been asked to tell what he or she would do in order to arrange an induced abortion,

---

[14]Georges Simmel, *Conflict and the Web of Group Affiliation,* trans. Kurt Wolff and Reinhard Bendix (Glencoe, Ill.: Free Press, 1955). See also unpublished papers by Ithiel Pool *et al.,* "Mathematical Models for Social Contact"; "Contact Nets"; Massachusetts Institute of Technology, 1965.

[15]Stanley Milgram, "The Small World Problem," *Psychology Today* vol. 1, no. 1 (May 1967).

and that all have given complete and honest answers to the question. Some would say that they would make contact with a particular abortionist known to them. Others would say that they would ask a person known by them to have such information. Still others might not have any specific information themselves, but would ask someone who might be more likely to have such information. Finally, some people would say that they do not know anything about it because they never had occasion to consider the problem; some of these would not consider arranging an abortion for any reason.

To interpret the results, imagine taking a very large map of the United States and plotting the location of all the abortionists named in the interviews. One would leave some space on the edge of the map to plot the location of abortionists outside the country who were named by the informants. Next, one would plot the location of those who named each of the abortionists, drawing a line to connect them to the one or more abortionists named. Then one would use a different color to plot the people who said they would ask someone whom they knew had access to an abortionist, or whom they thought might have access to an abortionist. Finally, one would plot the location of those who refused to entertain the question. One would not draw lines connecting them to anyone else, as they are not a part of the network of information about abortionists. When one finished with this hypothetical task (which could not possibly be completed in a single lifetime, even if the information could be obtained) one would have a complete inventory of the information on hand about how to arrange an abortion.

One would no doubt find that certain parts of the map were densely filled with lines, while other parts were relatively empty, reflecting both the distribution of population and regional differences in the use of abortion. If the map was not hopelessly cluttered with data, one would see a number of distinct networks of people connected directly or indirectly to an abortionist. There would be roughly the same number of distinct networks as there are practicing abortionists available to the population.[16] The size of these networks would vary a great deal, from a few people to an estimated one hundred thousand

[16]The number of networks will be "roughly" equal to the number of practicing abortionists because abortionists sometimes work in groups, or "mills" or "rings," which share a single referral system. See Jerome E. Bates, "The Abortion Mill: An Institutional Analysis," *Journal of Criminal Law, Criminology, and Police Science* 45 (July–August 1954) : 163.

who could directly reach one unusually well-known doctor who recently retired. Those who can directly reach the abortionist will usually include all his previous patients, usually a few friends or relatives of each patient who were told exactly where the abortion was performed, and anyone else who may have had occasion to learn the abortionist's location. The abortionist may have a referral system of his own, consisting of doctors, pharmacists, and others who come in contact with people seeking abortion. At the second step from the abortionist would be persons who know that someone in the first circle knows how to arrange an abortion, but who could not reach the abortionist directly. One would surely find some cases in which a single person names two or more abortionists or pathways to different abortionists, which link the various networks, and one would surely find some ineffective networks, composed of persons in contact with an abortionist who is no longer practicing, and some networks which are not connected to any abortionist at all. Some of the information plotted, then, must be wrong, representing an unworkable strategy that would not actually lead anyone to an abortionist.

As interesting as it would be to know the number of different networks, the size of the networks, and the proportion which are inoperative, this data collection has the built-in disadvantage that we have not asked people how they *do* arrange induced abortions—only how they might if they had occasion to do so. The picture is oversimplified, too, because people stop describing what they would do when they have discussed one possible avenue, whereas individuals who are actually searching for an abortionist may try and fail, try and fail again, and continue to try until they succeed.

In order to understand how these networks develop, how they change over time, and how people actually use them to obtain abortions, imagine that we had some way of knowing when people in the population talked with others about abortion, rather than collecting our information by having each person talk with an interviewer. To analyze the actual flow of communication about abortion, we should distinguish three different levels of information about abortion. First, there is the basic information that abortion exists as an alternative to unwanted pregnancies, along with factual information about how it is performed, what it costs, how dangerous it is, and so forth. This kind of information can be, and often is, communicated by the mass media as well as from person to person.

A second level of information is gossip about particular experiences and specific individuals. When one person tells another that a certain woman has had an abortion, whether she is identified by name or not, the recipient of the gossip has located a channel through which he or she may be able to locate an abortionist if the need ever arises. In addition, gossip may serve the function of making abortion an acceptable and comprehensible procedure to people who have not previously been involved in it.

On these first two levels, the initiative for the transmission of information lies with the person who has the information. On the third level, an actual search for an abortionist, the initiative lies with those who want the information. A pregnant woman, or someone acting in her interest, asks for the name, address, qualifications, and any necessary passwords or formulas that will enable her to reach a specific abortionist. The first request for help may lead to one of three consequences: she may be directed to an abortionist; she may be sent to ask another person who might have the information; or the request may lead to a dead end, not producing any useful suggestions. In the event of either of the last two possibilities, the sequence of asking for help may be repeated, and may continue to be repeated until an address is located. The number of people asked for help will usually not represent the entire universe of people that the woman could have asked for help. Instead the list is usually truncated by the location of one satisfactory channel to an abortionist. People who are asked for help and cannot or will not give help nevertheless are linked to the networks of communication about abortion by their knowledge that the person who asked them is about to have an abortion. When a successful search is completed and the abortion is carried out, the woman becomes a part of the network of "her" abortionist and all her acquaintances who learn about the abortion experience in any way, by being asked to help or by hearing gossip about her experience, become more distant nodes in the same network.

These networks are formed and modified over time, therefore, as the unplanned result of individuals' attempts to solve their own problems. Through actual searches to terminate an already existing unwanted pregnancy and through gossip about people who obtain abortions, the information necessary to make it possible to locate abortionists in the future is diffused and brought up to date as abortionists enter and leave abortion practices and change their addresses. Because information circulates selectively, primarily among intimate friends and age-mates, closely adjacent people may have access to quite different amounts of information. Young women enter the period of life when they may seek abortion at a time when few of their friends have had occasion to learn of a source. Similarly, other people come to a time in life when none of their acquaintances require the service of abortionists, either because of the passing of the reproductive period, because skill with contraception largely reduces the probability of unwanted pregnancies, or because they are happy to have children at that stage of life. The need to locate an abortionist is a rare enough event in most circles of acquaintances that persons may gather and use information at one point in time only to find on the next occasion when it is required that it is entirely out of date and that the search must be conducted all over again. Networks of referral may and often do persist for many years after the abortionist has stopped practicing as a result of death or retirement or arrest.

This procedure has some built-in advantages for those involved. There is some basis, although perhaps not as much as one might wish, for mutual trust between the seekers and those they are asking for help. The person asked for help usually has no financial motive for distorting the truth concerning any facilities he or she may know about. It is often possible for the woman to get in touch with someone who previously went to the abortionist being discussed, to get a first-hand account of the kind of treatment offered, the kind of person the abortionist seems to be, and the costs involved.

The networks of informal contacts described function to provide most women with satisfactory abortions—not satisfactory by the usual standards expected of medical care but acceptable to them for an illegal procedure. As an individual response to unwanted pregnancy, the present system of illegal abortion is at least quiet and inconspicuous. The principle of refusing abortion is maintained on the law books, while millions evade the principle on their own initiative. The system, if such an ephemeral form of social organization can be called a system, is not an efficient one. The location of a qualified or unqualified abortionist, expensive or cheap, nearby or far away, is largely a matter of whom one chooses to ask and the recent history of abortion experiences known to the people who are asked. One finds New York women flying to Puerto Rico to reach the only abortionist they learn about, while Puerto Rican women are flying to New York to follow up the leads they have found. Poor women sometimes put themselves deeply in debt to pay for expensive abortions, while wealthy women are sometimes unable to find the highly skilled practitioners they can afford to pay.

The costs of the contradiction between the widely accepted principle that abortion should not be freely available to those who want it and the widespread evasion of the principle are paid by the men and women directly involved. These costs—of money, of fear, of lack of social control over abortionists, of anxiety and guilt, of risk of injury and death—are unequally distributed over the population of abortion seekers and abortionists. Some pay a great deal, some only a little. There is little justice and little predictability in the allocation of these costs.

The bulk of this book consists of an investigation of the concrete properties of some aspects of the social structure of abortion. The channels of communication which permit abortion seekers to reach abortionists are not the whole structure of the abortion situation in America. The recruitment of abortionists, relations between different abortionists and between individual abortionists and their employees, relations between abortionists and the police, and so on, are also important parts of the social structure. The present study is focused upon the actual searches undertaken by individuals who have had abortions, and little information has been gathered on the more formal aspects of the structure. The informal aspects of the system are investigated through the accounts of their own experience given by women who have had abortions, along with the circumstances of conception, the reasons the pregnancies were rejected, the various persons who aided and hindered the women in carrying out their wishes, and the long- and short-term aftereffects of the abortion experience. In a final chapter, the types of abortions the women obtained will be discussed in terms of the factors that seem to lead some people to competently performed medical abortions, legal or illegal, while others find only poor facilities available.

One further aspect of the social structure of abortion should be emphasized before we turn to the conduct of the present study and the results of the study. Abortion is such a widespread and uncoordinated activity that there is a considerable danger of coming to grossly incorrect conclusions about the "usual" or "normal" state of events. In an ambiguous situation like this, it is normal to generalize from the experience of the persons one knows. In this case, however, people who accept abortion as a legitimate alternative to unwanted pregnancy are likely to be loosely linked to one another through mutual acquaintanceship. The presence among one's acquaintances of others who have had experience with abortion may encourage the use of abortion as a solution to the problem of unwanted pregnancy. Persons within such acquaintance networks will tend to overestimate the incidence of such experiences. Other circles of acquaintances, which do not include any members who are known to have had an abortion, will not provide their members with channels to abortionists, and will encourage the erroneous impression that abortion is much less prevalent than it, in fact, is.

This same phenomenon of selective perception of the picture can be seen in some more extreme cases. Psychiatrists will tend to overestimate the proportion of women who have psychiatric disorders following abortion, since they are sought out by those who do. Physicians and attendants in the emergency wards of large public hospitals will tend to overestimate the proportion of all abortions that end in serious injuries and infections. Persons involved in political groups for abortion-law reform will overestimate the proportion of women who are morally indignant at the injustice of the laws, and no doubt this study, based on a self-selected group of volunteers, tends to encourage overestimation of the proportion of women who are willing to talk about their experience with others.

Recognizing this tendency, one is of course still limited to the information available. Learning about the accessible cases will give a partial view of the total picture which, recognized as such, is far superior to no knowledge at all.

# 2

## *The Design of the Research*

To investigate the process of arranging abortions, it was necessary to locate and investigate some actual cases. I recognized from the very beginning that it would not be possible to make a complete and final study of all the variations used by people seeking abortions. A realistic set of goals was defined as: (1) to gain a complete account of exactly how some abortions were arranged, including all the persons asked for help, the reason why those particular persons were asked, what help or hindrance they gave, and the outcome of the search; (2) to investigate a large enough number of cases that the peculiarities of individual cases could be seen as such, permitting the overall patterns of similarities and differences to emerge; and (3) to carry out the investigation in such a way that the process of gathering information would not in any way harm those who gave information.

Two different strategies were considered as ways to gain the necessary information. One, called the "snowball" technique, has been found very useful in investigating other social phenomena which are based on personal networks.[1] The technique consists of gaining the cooperation of one or more persons who are considered "starting points." The starting-point person is asked to give a list of the persons with whom he or she is in contact by some criterion: for the purposes of this study, the criterion might be having asked for help in arranging an abortion, having talked about abortion, and so on. Each of those mentioned is then asked for a similar list of persons related to them by the same criterion. The network properties are investigated by following the network out to wherever it leads. Often one finds that after several steps the network leads back into itself, and one finds a relatively bounded group related in this way. The "snowball" technique was rejected for this research owing to the difficulties of gaining the trust and cooperation of each of the persons in the network. Without such cooperation the research would be impossible. It was also felt that there might be legal dangers in accumulating the necessary lists of names and addresses of specific people who are related to one another through participation in an illegal activity.

The strategy adopted instead was to gain the cooperation of only one informant in each of a larger number of cases of abortion. The decision was made to accept information only from women who had had an abortion performed recently enough that they could remember the events in detail. The woman involved was chosen as the one person most likely to know all the details of how the abortion was arranged and performed. It was important that this research should not become an occasion of betrayal of secrets: the woman involved was considered the "owner" of the information that an abortion was performed, free to give or withhold information as she chose. To reduce the possibility that the study would harm or upset the informants, guidelines of recruitment and data collection were established. First, no pressure was put on any woman to contribute to the study: no financial inducements were offered; all the women were given an opportunity to decline to participate by simply not taking the action of making contact with me or not sending in a questionnaire; and no pursuit of potential informants was made. Personal friends and friends of acquaintances were mildly discouraged from volunteering, to coun-

[1]For an example of successful use of the "snowball" technique on a less personal research question, see Nicholas Mullins, "Social Foundations of Informal Communication in the Biological Sciences" (Ph.D. diss., Harvard University, 1966).

teract any undue personal pressure to volunteer, although enthusiastic volunteers were accepted. Women who had attempted to arrange abortions and had not succeeded were not accepted, as I felt that the psychological problems of discussing an attempt to terminate a pregnancy which produced a living child were too difficult to handle. Psychiatrists and psychiatric clinics were rejected as possible sources of contacts with women, to reduce the possibility of reaching women who had been seriously disturbed by their experience and might be further disturbed by talking about it.

At the outset of the research, it was hoped that a quota sample could be obtained, consisting of a certain number of women, married and unmarried, well educated and moderately educated, under thirty years of age and over thirty, and white and nonwhite. The difficulties of recruitment made this plan impractical. All volunteers were accepted who met the criterion of having had one or more deliberate abortions, whether legally or illegally performed, who came forward to offer information in a way that indicated that they were freely offering their help, and who were able to give a full and coherent account of their experience.

## Channels of Recruitment

The problem of recruiting volunteers to tell of their experience is similar in some ways to the problem of the women searching for an abortionist: that is, how to locate a person on the basis of a characteristic by which he or she does not wish to be publicly known. It is fortunate that I did not share their problem of working under a six-to-ten-week deadline, since I did not succeed in reaching any volunteers within the first ten weeks of the data collection.

The plan was to get in contact with a number of different people or agencies in regular communication with a range of women in some context where the fact that the women had had abortions might be known: physicians, birth-control clinics, and abortion-law lobbying groups seemed to be the obvious possibilities.

The first task in starting the data collection, therefore, was to approach some of the people who have publicly indicated an interest in the problem of abortion in America by their published writing, by participation in conferences on abortion, or by their membership in abortion-law reform groups. Introductions were obtained to such people wherever possible. If an introduction could not be arranged, a letter was sent explaining the goals of the research, the procedure proposed, and something of my qualifications to carry out the research, and asking for advice and help in recruitment. A sample of the kind of letter sent is in the appendix.[2] Whenever the source person indicated interest in the research, the letter was followed by a personal visit to discuss it in more detail, if possible. Over the course of the data collection, about 150 letters were written, twenty of which were followed up by personal visits. The results of these efforts were uneven. For example, the first few physicians I obtained introductions to were not directly helpful: they did not feel that they could use their special relationship with their patients to encourage participation in such a study. At the same time, a prominent obstetrician heard of the study through casual discussions with a Harvard researcher and offered me his assistance. He was instrumental in arranging for several volunteers to communicate with me, and personally approached three colleagues whom he thought might be helpful.

Three birth-control clinics were asked for help. In each case, an introduction to the director of the clinic was arranged before the meeting. The director of the first clinic was interested in the research but unable to offer any help; the second was willing to try to recruit volunteers but had no success among the clients, and the third provided contact with a large number of volunteers.

Two abortion-law reform groups were approached. The first was not willing to attempt to recruit volunteers but made several useful suggestions as to people who might be helpful. The second group, in California, provided a list of its members who live on the East Coast so that they could be asked to help recruit volunteers and distributed a large number of questionnaires among its California members. Two other political organizations heard of the study, apparently from members of the California group, and distributed questionnaire forms which they obtained from the California group.

Three abortionists were encountered in the search for volunteers. One of these heard of the study from an unknown second party and approached me to offer help. Introductions to the other two were provided by people I had asked for help. Each of the abortionists had indicated that he would be interested in helping before I made con-

[2]The letters to individuals and agencies were individually typed, following the model which is reproduced in the Appendix to give an idea of the form of the request. Letters written to physicians, social scientists, and birth-control clinic staffs were similar but differed in details of emphasis.

tact with him. One of these was willing to discuss his practice but was not willing to ask his patients to contribute to the study. The other two were willing to inform certain patients whom they thought would be likely to help. One referred several patients over the course of six months and the other referred numerous current and past patients. These abortionists are all physicians. As one would expect from the fact that they exposed themselves to a certain amount of risk in order to help in a study, they have more than an average sense of their social responsibility in the conduct of abortion and considerable interest in the well-being of patients. The information they gave on the conduct of their own practice was useful in gaining a perspective on the accounts given by the women, although it is recognized that they are by no means typical of the abortionists who practice in America.

Others who were asked for advice and help in recruitment were physicians, especially specialists in obstetrics and gynecology; demographers and sociologists who have worked in the area of reproductive behavior of American families; journalists who have written about the problems of abortion; and individuals who have made a special point of informing themselves on the availability of abortionists in order to help anyone who comes to them.

The search for contacts with potential volunteers was frustrating. No agencies were located which could be used as a systematic source for recruiting volunteers. In fact, there is no class of agency in our society which has both the kind of relationship with a wide range of women that would permit abortion to be discussed *and* the kind of relationship to research organizations that would permit these relationships to be used to increase public knowledge.[3] On the other hand, there are particular individuals, some of whom are physicians or executives of birth-control clinics or members of abortion-law reform organizations, who have a close relationship with a number of women and who are interested in promoting research in this area for their own reasons. The recruitment process was necessarily ad hoc rather than systematic. The vast majority of approaches on my part did not lead directly to any volunteers. On the other hand, some volunteers were found as a result of these efforts toward recruitment, and a

[3]For a discussion of a similar research problem involving a demanding and highly personal request to the participants which was resolved in a similar way, see Elizabeth Bott, *Family and Social Network* (London: Tavistock Publications, 1959), especially pp. 12-16.

number of fruitful sources of contacts were people who were not directly asked for help, but who heard of the study from people who were asked for help. Ultimately 114 women volunteered to contribute to the study as a result, however indirect, of the contacts made with agencies.

Table 1 presents a summary of the number of agencies and individuals approached in the attempt to recruit volunteers, the number who agreed to try to find at least one potential volunteer, and the numbers of women who volunteered via these various sources.

TABLE 1

AGENCIES APPROACHED AND INFORMANTS REACHED
THROUGH THESE SOURCES

| Type of Agency | Agency | | Respondents | |
| | N Approached | N that Agreed to Try to Help | Inter- views | Question- naire |
|---|---|---|---|---|
| Birth-Control Clinics | 3 | 2 | 0 | 23 |
| Physicians, especially Obstetrics- Gynecology | 12 | 4 | 7 | 6 |
| Abortionists | 3 | 2 | 1 | 15 |
| Political organizations to change the laws on abortion | 3 | 4 | 0 | 31 |
| Personal letters to members of one such organization | 100 | 10 | 7 | 0 |
| Contacts established by volunteers in the study | 0 | 0 | 5 | 14 |
| Volunteers who heard about the study through casual discussions and volunteered directly | — | — | 5 | 0 |
| Other requests      approx. | 25 | 3 | 0 | 0 |
| Total      approx. | 150 | 25 | 25 | 89 |

Note: Total participants 25 + 89 = 114

## The Data Collection

### Interviewing Procedures

The people who agreed to help with recruitment of volunteers were asked to approach women they knew who had already mentioned having had an abortion. They were asked not to make special inquiry about abortion to women who had not mentioned it, to avoid giving potential volunteers the impression that they were being pursued for their action. In cases where a woman had already mentioned a deliberate abortion, they were asked to tell the woman about the study and to give her my name, address, and telephone number if she were interested in participating.

The first contact with a volunteer, therefore, came when she wrote a letter or telephoned. Women who lived on the East Coast but outside of Boston were encouraged to telephone collect to my home. When a woman phoned, or when I phoned her in response to her letter, I thanked her for her cooperation, answered any questions she might have, and made arrangements for a meeting, usually within a few days to a week of the time she called. In most cases, we agreed to meet at the woman's home during an evening or weekend. A few of the interviews took place at my office, two at my home, two at offices offered by the person who arranged the contact, and five were conducted in restaurants when no other suitable place could be arranged.

The first ten interviews were entirely open-ended and were recorded on a portable tape recorder, with the permission of the woman.[4] In the first few minutes of the interview, the goal of the research was described as finding out how a woman makes the decision to seek an abortion and exactly how she manages to carry out that decision. The women were asked to tell about all the events that had any bearing on the abortion. Each woman was asked to make a point of not mentioning the names of the persons involved, even though we would be talking about individuals. With some women, it was convenient to use first names in our discussions; others found it easier to refer to people by their relationships as "my doctor," "my mother," "my girlfriend from work." In the first interviews, the women were asked simply to start from the beginning, when the pregnancy occurred, and tell what happened, leaving me to ask questions when the events were not clear. A great deal of repetition and checking was necessary in these early interviews to make sure that the full sequence of events had been covered.

The recordings of the first interviews were used as the basis for a series of drafts of interviewing outlines, to work out a format flexible

[4]I would like to express my warm appreciation particularly to these ten women, who were extremely cooperative in answering questions and in permitting their answers to be recorded.

enough to cover the range of experiences that different people reported and systematic enough to insure that important aspects of the experience would not be neglected. By the eleventh interview, a standard form was developed for guiding the interview and recording the information: all the subsequent interviews were conducted without tape-recording.

All the women who were interviewed were pleasantly frank about their experiences.[5] Although the women were told that they were free to refuse to answer any questions that they considered too personal, none declined to answer any. I found that the tension of the situation was reduced by mentioning early in our discussion that I knew there had been an abortion. When a woman expressed embarrassment by talking in generalities about her experience, a specific question which suggested that I knew about the concrete alternatives she faced usually reduced the tension and made it possible for her to continue discussing her experience in a matter-of-fact way. Most of the women had long before concluded that they had done the best they could in the circumstances, and did not feel it necessary to justify their behavior to me. A few of the women were still quite concerned about whether they had done the right thing and wanted to discuss their emotional reactions to the situation. I felt a heavy responsibility to these women not to leave them more upset about their experience than they had been before our discussion. I listened to what they had to say and sincerely sympathized with their difficulties: my presence may have helped them put their experiences into perspective by reminding them that other women have faced the same problems. In general, my attitude toward the information gained in the interviews was matter-of-fact and nonjudgmental. At the close of an interview, I thanked the woman for the cooperation given and assured her that she had been very helpful. These interviews lasted from forty-five minutes to three and a half hours.

The twenty-five interviews provided invaluable information in a form that could be checked and rechecked and put into the context of the real-life situation in which it occurred. Nevertheless, there are disadvantages to relying entirely upon interviews for such a study.

[5]Refusal to answer specific questions was very rare among the women who volunteered, although some answered personal questions very briefly, without discussing their feelings about the matter. Many offered a great deal of background information about their experience which was not directly requested, both in the interviews and in letters accompanying the questionnaire form.

The number of interviews which can be collected in a given period is limited by the time consumed, both for the informants and for me. Interviews tended to be expensive, owing to telephone calls and the frequent necessity for an all-day trip, usually to New York or New Haven from Boston. Most important, there are many women who would be glad to participate in such a study who are not willing to agree to a personal meeting with a stranger. For these reasons, questionnaires were prepared and printed on the basis of the information gained in the interviews in October, 1966.

### Questionnaire Procedures

Questionnaires are in some ways superior to interviews for collecting information for a study like this one. Agencies in touch with women who have had abortions can offer such women questionnaires, rather than asking them to communicate with the researcher. If the woman does not wish to participate, she can refuse the questionnaire or accept it and throw it away later. There is less opportunity to put pressure on her to participate, and there is less reason why she should want to refuse.

One difficulty with questionnaires is that questions cannot be introduced as they naturally arise in the course of a discussion, but must be fully laid out for inspection before the woman even begins the task of completing it. The way the questions are phrased cannot be modified to suit the style in which the woman speaks, which tends to alienate some women no matter how the questions are put. Finally, one never knows who will be given a questionnaire form and try to fill it out. For this reason, the questionnaire has an introductory section concerning birth control and abortion which can be completed by any person who happens to get it. The bulk of the questionnaire, of course, concerns personal experience with abortion. The questions concerning the other persons consulted at various stages of the process are a major part of the questionnaire, but unfortunately tend to be answered in less detail in the questionnaire than in the interviews. A copy of the questionnaire form is in the appendix: readers interested in the details of the information requested may wish to turn to this form before reading the results reported.

Questionnaire forms were furnished to the same agencies that had been helpful in finding women for interviews, and in addition, to some agencies that were willing to help find potential volunteers but that were located well outside the Boston area. Approximately one thousand copies were sent out to these agencies between October 1966 and March 1967. The number of copies of the questionnaire actually given to women eligible for the study is not known: presumably many copies, perhaps the majority, never left the offices to which they were sent. By March 1967, when the data collection was closed to permit tabulation of results, about 150 copies had been completed and returned. Some of these had been filled out by women who had not had personal experience with abortion, and some were too incomplete to be usable. Eighty-nine questionnaires were completed by women who had had one or more abortions. These eighty-nine returns, along with the twenty-five interviews, make up the population on which this study is based.

The questionnaire form is long and is difficult to complete. No doubt many of the women who were given a form would have been willing to answer a few questions about their experience, but did not have the motivation to complete this time-consuming task. The opportunity to gain a small amount of information from these women was sacrificed in the interest of gaining information comparable to that obtained in interviews. While the return rate was low, the degree of cooperation from those who did participate was very high. Less than a third of the usable returns consisted only of brief answers to the questions asked. Most of the women wrote sufficient explanatory material to give a clear impression of what happened. Sixteen took the suggestion in the instructions to the questionnaire and wrote an additional letter or series of comments which was enclosed. Many added notes to the effect that they hoped that something would be done to make abortion safer for all women, thanking me for my interest in "this much neglected problem."

# 3

## *The Characteristics of the Volunteers*

In order to protect the privacy of the women who gave the information, it is not possible to present individual cases in detail. It is not enough to withhold names to protect the informants: a description consisting of a woman's place of residence, her marital status, her religion, education, and occupation would be sufficient in many cases to identify the woman to those who happen to know her. Disguising her identity by changing the description defeats the whole purpose of research: one cannot test hypotheses on the connection between social characteristics and behavior if one cannot trust the accuracy of the description. The descriptions presented are accurate rather than fictionalized, but will be presented as the distribution of traits within the study group.

The following three chapters consist of a summary of the experiences of this group of women when they had their abortions. This chapter is devoted to an introduction to the women as they were at the time of the study.

On the average, about four years elapsed from the time of the first abortion the woman ever had until the time of the study. Some women have had more than one abortion, but their first is the one reported in detail in this study. This four-year average represents a compromise between the forty-two women who had their first abortion within a year of the time they contributed to the study (sixteen, in fact, had undergone abortion with the two weeks preceding their participation), and those who had their first abortion some time ago. Almost all the women had had an abortion since 1960: some of them had their first experience with abortion before that date.

## Age and Marital Status

The ages of the women who contributed to the study range between seventeen, a girl still in high school, and fifty-two, a woman who obtained an abortion for a menopausal pregnancy a few years ago. Most are in their twenties at the present time. Table 2 shows the cross-tabulation of age and marital state.

TABLE 2

CURRENT AGE AND MARITAL STATUS OF THE STUDY GROUP

| Age | Single | | Married | | Marital Status Previously Married | | Total | Percent |
|---|---|---|---|---|---|---|---|---|
| | N | Percent* | N | Percent* | N | Percent* | | |
| 17–20 | 12 | 21 | 1 | 3 | 1 | 4 | 14 | 12.3 |
| 21–25 | 28 | 49 | 9 | 29 | 2 | 8 | 39 | 34.2 |
| 26–30 | 14 | 25 | 4 | 13 | 12 | 46 | 30 | 26.3 |
| 31–35 | 2 | 4 | 8 | 26 | 3 | 12 | 13 | 11.4 |
| 36–40 | 0 | 0 | 5 | 16 | 5 | 19 | 10 | 8.8 |
| 40 plus | 1 | 2 | 4 | 13 | 3 | 12 | 8 | 7.0 |
| | | 100 | | 100 | | 100 | | 100.0 |
| Total | 57 | | 31 | | 26 | | 114 | |
| | (50.0%) | | (27.2%) | | (22.8%) | | | |

Note* Columns may not sum to 100 owing to rounding of percentages.

Half the women are single, and five are engaged to be married soon. Less than a third are currently married, and some of these had their experience with abortion before their marriage. The previously married group, twenty-six women, includes seven who are separated from their husbands and do not expect to reestablish the marriage, eighteen who are divorced, and one who is widowed.

## Household Composition

All the married women live with their husbands, and slightly more than half have children in the home as well. Single women live alone (twenty-two), share a house or apartment with female roommates (eighteen), live at home with their parental families (nine), live with their boyfriends (five), or live in college dormitories or sorority houses (three). Of the twenty-six previously married women, fifteen live with their children, and two of these are living with a man as well as their children. Six others live alone, another has a roommate and two have returned to live in their parental homes.

## Residence

Almost all the women who contributed to the study are urban dwellers. Fifty-one lived in New York City at the time of the study, fourteen in Boston, thirteen in San Francisco, and nine in the Los Angeles area. The others are spread across the country—in Pennsyvania, Connecticut, New Jersey, Michigan, Washington, D.C., Oklahoma, Oregon, and California. One woman, living in England, reported on an abortion obtained in the United States.

## Education

Most of the women are well educated. There are ten who have postgraduate degrees on the masters or doctoral level, and nineteen more have started but not completed an advanced degree. All but twenty-one of the women have had at least some college education. Table 3 presents the educational attainments of the group in detail. Thirty-three of the women do not consider themselves finished with their formal education, although only twenty-one of these were enrolled in full-time studies at the time they contributed to the study.

## Occupation

The characteristic which gives the most information about the day-to-day life of these women is occupation. Table 4 presents in detail the occupations they named. One notes that the common occupations of women—housewife, teacher, nurse, and secretary—are well represented. The group differs from the population as a whole in that more of the women hold paying jobs and that more of these are high-status jobs which require considerable education and initiative.

TABLE 3

HIGHEST LEVEL OF EDUCATION COMPLETED
AT TIME OF DATA COLLECTION

| Highest Level Completed | Number |
|---|---|
| Grade school only (eight years) | 1 |
| Some high school | 2 |
| Completed high school | 10 |
| High school plus vocational training | 8 |
| Some college | 36 |
| College graduate | 28 |
| Some postgraduate education | 19 |
| Finished graduate school (M.A., M.D., Ph.D.) | 10 |
| Total | 114 |

TABLE 4

OCCUPATIONS REPORTED BY INFORMANTS
(HELD AT THE TIME OF DATA COLLECTION)

| Occupation | Number | Percent |
|---|---|---|
| Housewives | 13 | 11.4 |
|   Housewife (8), housewife and mother (3), housewife with a part-time job (2) | | |
| Students | 21 | 18.4 |
|   College student (12), graduate student (5), high-school student, secretarial-school student, professional-school student, nursing-school student | | |
| Professionals, managers, and proprietors | 22 | 19.3 |
|   Elementary-school teacher (6), social worker (5), high-school teacher (2), editor (2), physician, lawyer, architect, biochemist, librarian, business executive, owns own business | | |
| Artistic and creative occupations—"glamor jobs" | 13 | 11.4 |
|   Artist (painter and sculptor) (3), actress (2), fashion model (2), journalist (2), commercial artist or illustrator (2), writer (novelist, poet) (2) | | |
| Skilled service occupations | 12 | 10.5 |
|   Nurse (5), medical secretary (2), medical research assistant (2), medical technician, dental technician, stewardess | | |
| Secretarial and clerical workers | 28 | 24.6 |
|   Secretary (12), executive secretary (7), clerical workers (5), sales (2), bookkeeper, bank clerk | | |
| Semiskilled workers | 5 | 4.4 |
|   Waitress (2), telephone operator, dry-cleaning worker, multiple-part-time jobs | | |
| Total | 114 | 100.0 |

The occupations and the educational attainment of these women suggest that the group as a whole has a high level of ability and that the women have had a high level of opportunity during their lives. There are special problems in assigning social class designations to women: it is usually necessary to take their fathers' or their husbands' characteristics into account to make a realistic judgment. There are additional problems in judging social class for people of either sex during their teens and twenties, when they may not yet have reached the level of achievement consistent with their style of life. The majority of this group of women are at least temporarily independent of both fathers and husbands. On the basis of their own social characteristics, we can describe the 30 percent of the women in professional, managerial, proprietary, artistic, and creative occupations, and most of the students, as being upper middle-class; the thirty-five percent in skilled service, secretarial, and clerical occupations as middle-class; and the less than five percent in semiskilled work as lower-middle or working-class. Using education as the criterion, one might be inclined to include twenty-one of the women, those who have not had any college education, in the lower status group.

It is clear that even though social class categories have a very limited usefulness when applied to this group of women, the group is heavily biased toward the higher end of the social class continuum. This observation does not mean that lower-class or working-class women do not get abortions: it only shows that few such women volunteered for this study. It does mean that caution is needed in interpreting the results of this study. The study group is dominated by the middle- and upper-class women who volunteered to contribute and the results should be interpreted as such.

## Religion

Thirty-nine of the women said that they had no religion or were atheists or agnostics. Those who referred to themselves as Protestant (thirty-five), Catholic (eleven), and Jewish (twenty-six) usually also indicated that they are not active members of any church or synagogue. Only eight women are active churchgoers and an additional thirteen are nominal members, grouped together as "active" in table 5.

It is fair to say that the study group is not religious. It is not fair

TABLE 5

RELIGIOUS AFFILIATION AND DEGREE OF ACTIVITY

| Religious Group | Not Active N | Active N | N | Total Percent |
|---|---|---|---|---|
| Catholic | 8 | 3 | 11 | 9.7 |
| Protestant | 23 | 12 | 35 | 30.7 |
| Jewish | 21 | 5 | 26 | 22.8 |
| None and other groups* | 41 | 1 | 42 | 36.8 |
|  | 93 | 21 | 114 | 100.0% |
| Total | 81.6% | 18.4% | | |

*Other religious groups mentioned are Christian Science, Bahai, and Zen Buddhism, each named by one woman.

to take this finding as indicating anything about the churchgoing behavior of all women who obtain abortions. The findings may be an artifact of the recruitment process or it may be that women who do not have religious conflicts about abortion found it easier to volunteer.

## Attitudes toward Abortion

A recent national study on attitudes toward legalization of abortion permits placing the study group within the framework of the national population. Rossi (1966) surveyed a random sample of the United States adult population on their attitudes toward legalization of abortion under a number of conditions. Table 6 summarizes the overall findings, based on the answers given by approximately fifteen hundred adults.

A similar group of hypothetical cases was presented to the study population, to ask whether they would approve of abortion being granted. As might be expected, these women were extremely liberal in giving their approval.

Comparing Rossi's results with table 7, we see that the women who participated in the present study are considerably more permissive than the national average on the question of legal abortion. The national survey indicated that men tend to be more permissive in their attitudes toward abortion than women, and more highly educated people of both sexes are consistently more permissive than less educated people. Men retain their lead in permissiveness, according to Rossi, at each level of education. The finding that women are less permissive of abortion than men is attributed to the greater frequency of church attendance and participation among women.

TABLE 6

ATTITUDES OF THE GENERAL POPULATION
TOWARD LEGAL ABORTION UNDER SPECIFIED CONDITIONS*

Question: Please tell me whether or not you think it should be possible for a pregnant woman to obtain a legal abortion (followed by the conditions specified below).

| | Percentages | | Don't |
| --- | --- | --- | --- |
| | Yes | No | Know |
| 1. If the woman's own health is endangered by the pregnancy | 71 | 26 | 3 |
| 2. If she became pregnant as a result of rape | 56 | 38 | 6 |
| 3. If there is a strong chance of serious defect in the baby | 55 | 41 | 4 |
| 4. If the family has a very low income and cannot afford any more children | 21 | 77 | 2 |
| 5. If she is not married and does not want to marry the man | 18 | 80 | 2 |
| 6. If she is married and does not want any more children | 15 | 83 | 2 |

N = approximately 1,500

*From Alice Rossi, "Public Views on Abortion" (unpublished paper, National Opinion Research Center, February, 1966).

Rossi's study indicates that religious membership and degree of participation are strongly related to attitudes toward abortion in the population as a whole. At the low levels of educational attainment (less than a high-school degree), both Catholics and Protestants show very little permissiveness on abortion, while Jews and agnostics are much more permissive. With increasing education, Protestants are found to increase in acceptance of abortion, while Catholics do not vary by educational level. At the level of some college education or more, a scant majority of the Protestants approve in all cases listed in table 6, along with a considerable majority of Jews and agnostics, while the proportion of Catholics who approve in all cases is only about 30 percent, hardly different from the group who finished elementary school or less. The high degree of permissiveness found in the study group in association with a low level of religious membership and participation and a high level of education is consistent with the findings of the national study. This finding suggests that the study group has been drawn primarily from one extreme of the national range.

The third major factor that Rossi found associated with attitudes

TABLE 7

ATTITUDES OF THE STUDY GROUP
TOWARD LEGAL ABORTION UNDER SPECIFIED CONDITIONS

Question: Here is a list of some of the reasons
that people might have for wanting to interrupt
a pregnancy. If you think it is a good reason,
and you would approve of their decision, circle
"yes" after the reason. If you would not approve, just circle "no."

| | Response | | |
|---|---|---|---|
| | Yes | No | No Answer |
| 1. If the pregnancy endangered the mother's health | 113 | 0 | 1 |
| 2. If the woman wasn't married | 110 | 1 | 3 |
| 3. If the mother had taken drugs and the child might be deformed | 110 | 1 | 3 |
| 4. If the girl is under 16 years old | 108 | 2 | 4 |
| 5. If the couple thinks they cannot afford an-other child | 96 | 15 | 3 |
| 6. If a married couple didn't want another child at that time | 93 | 17 | 4 |
| | N = 114 | | |

toward legal abortion is general permissiveness toward premarital
sexual relations. The question used to measure this attitude was:

A woman has intimate relations with a man she is engaged to and
intends to marry. Is this: (1) Always or almost always wrong?
(2) Wrong only sometimes? (3) Probably all right?

Men were found to be generally more permissive about premarital
sexual relations under these circumstances than women. There were
no differences between men and women among those who held re-
strictive views on sex as to the acceptability of legal abortion, but
among those with permissive views of sex, men were found to be
more inclined than women to support legal abortion. Attitudes toward
premarital sex were found to be related to permissiveness toward
legal abortion not only in the specific cases which involve a premarital pregnancy, but in all the situations proposed.

Although the study group is extremely permissive concerning abortion, it is not a free and casual topic of conversation for them. Almost all the women named some persons with whom they would not
bring up the topic or with whom they would be uncomfortable if the

topic were brought up by others. Only two of the women said that they had never discussed it with anyone, but 40 percent of the respondents said that abortion is an extremely rare topic of conversation and others indicated that it is rare to mention it unless there was a specific need to find an abortionist for someone, or that it is a rare topic in general but is freely discussed within a certain circle of friends. Only 8 percent said that abortion is a common topic of conversation. For most of the women, abortion seems to be a subject which is rarely discussed, and then only in an intimate atmosphere with fairly close friends.

## Personal Histories

A woman's sexual and reproductive career can be summarized by her age at beginning sexual intercourse, the duration of that sexual relationship, and the dates and durations of any subsequent sexual relationships. Pregnancies can be located as occurring at a particular point in the woman's life and at a particular point in the sexual relationships she engages in. The women in the study group vary considerably in the length of time they have been exposed to the risk of pregnancy and in the number of pregnancies they have experienced. Figure 1 is an attempt to show the variations in sexual and reproductive history of a portion of the study group, merely to demonstrate the concept of a sexual and reproductive career.

To read figure 1, consider each of the numbered lines as the diagram of an actual woman's experience. Sexual initiation is represented by the first short vertical line; years of exposure outside of marriage are represented by a solid horizontal line; and years of exposure in marriage are expressed by a double line. Pregnancies which ended in a live birth are represented by a small circle on the line at the point in the woman's life when they occurred, while induced abortions are represented by an $x$ and spontaneous abortions by a $v$. The final short vertical line represents the point in the woman's life when she contributed to this study.

Line 1 should be read as a young woman who had her first sexual experience at the age of eighteen, continued to run the risk of pregnancy outside of marriage, conceived at twenty-three, and terminated the pregnancy by an induced abortion within a year of the time she participated in this study. To take another example, the woman described by line 4 experienced two premarital pregnancies in rapid succession after her sexual initiation at the age of twenty. She married

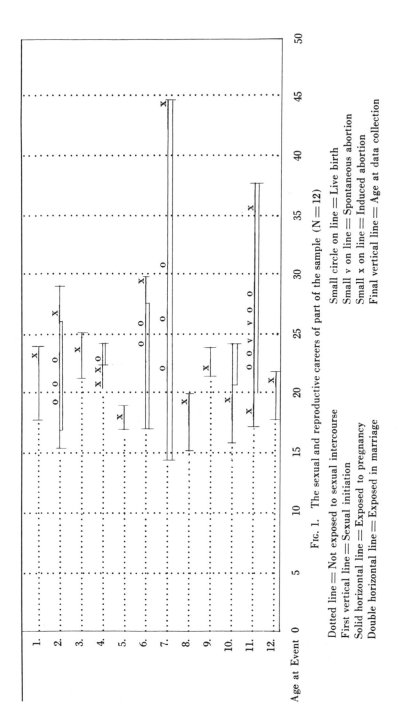

Fig. 1.  The sexual and reproductive careers of part of the sample (N = 12)

Age at Event

Dotted line = Not exposed to sexual intercourse
First vertical line = Sexual initiation
Solid horizontal line = Exposed to pregnancy
Double horizontal line = Exposed in marriage

Small circle on line = Live birth
Small v on line = Spontaneous abortion
Small x on line = Induced abortion
Final vertical line = Age at data collection

at twenty-two and had a live birth at twenty-three. She has had no more pregnancies and remains married at twenty-four, when she contributed to the study. The woman represented by line 6 married at the age of eighteen, and had her first child at twenty-four and her second child at twenty-six. The marriage ended in divorce when she was twenty-eight. At thirty, she conceived again and terminated the pregnancy by abortion. She was slightly over thirty when she volunteered for this study.

Sexual initiation occurred between the ages of twelve and twenty-six for the women in the study group. The mean age at sexual initiation was nineteen: about 10 percent started having intercourse before they were sixteen, and 10 percent after the age of twenty-two.

All the women were asked whether they had spent any time away from their parental homes prior to their marriage, if any. Only 11 percent of the women went directly from their parental homes to their marital homes, and only an additional 5 percent are still living with their parents. The rest of the women report having left their parental homes between the ages of eight and twenty-five. The ten women who left home between the ages of eight and fourteen were generally attending boarding school, although one woman, now twenty, had an unfortunate home life and left to work as a live-in baby-sitter at the age of twelve, attending school in the community of her employers. Most of the women left home between the ages of seventeen and nineteen to go to college or to work in another city. About 60 percent have had between two and eight years of "bachelor" life at the present time. Many are not married yet, so that if the same question were asked at the time of their marriage or the end of their reproductive life, the mean number of years would be somewhat higher than the 5.7 years reported at the present time.

The age at leaving their parental homes tended to coincide with the time of sexual initiation for these women. About 30 percent had their first sexual experience before leaving their parental homes, and 70 percent after. For this highly educated group of women, sexual initiation is not particularly related to the age at finishing formal education. Seventy percent of the women continued their education after sexual initiation; for 10 percent of the women the two events occurred in the same year; and 15 percent started having sexual intercourse only after their education was completed. For most women in the population the two events may tend to be more closely related than in the study group, as the beginning of sexual experience may tend to limit education for women who are unwilling or unable to resort to abortion to terminate unwanted pregnancies that may result.

All together, the 114 women have had 261 pregnancies, counting all abortions, live births, and spontaneous abortions or miscarriages. The married and previously married women, while making up only half the group, contribute the great majority of the pregnancies and slightly more than half the abortions. Table 8 presents the exact numbers of pregnancies and abortions experienced by the single, married, and previously married women.

TABLE 8

NUMBER OF PREGNANCIES AND ABORTIONS,
BY CURRENT MARITAL STATUS

| | Marital Status | | | |
| Number of Pregnancies | Single | Married | Previously Married | Total |
|---|---|---|---|---|
| 1 | 45 | 11 | 4 | 60 |
| 2 | 10 | 3 | 5 | 18 |
| 3 | 1 | 5 | 8 | 14 |
| 4 | 0 | 4 | 4 | 8 |
| 5 | 1 | 1 | 2 | 4 |
| 6 | 0 | 3 | 1 | 4 |
| 7 | 0 | 2 | 1 | 3 |
| 8 | 0 | 2 | 0 | 2 |
| 9 | 0 | 0 | 0 | 0 |
| 10 | 0 | 0 | 1 | 1 |
| Number of Women | 57 | 31 | 26 | 114 |
| Number of Pregnancies | 73 | 101 | 87 | 261 |
| Number of Abortions | Single | Married | Previously Married | Total |
| 1 | 47 | 22 | 17 | 86 |
| 2 | 8 | 7 | 4 | 19 |
| 3 | 1 | 2 | 4 | 7 |
| 4 | 1 | 0 | 0 | 1 |
| 5 | 0 | 0 | 1 | 1 |
| Number of Women | 57 | 31 | 26 | 114 |
| Number of Abortions | 70 | 42 | 42 | 154 |
| Percent of Pregnancies Terminated by Abortion | 96% | 42% | 48% | 59% |

Table 9 shows the cross-tabulation of the order of the pregnancy and the type of termination. Note that the first abortion is also the first pregnancy for 84 of the 114 women.

TABLE 9

PREGNANCY ORDER BY TYPE OF TERMINATION

| | Type of Termination | | | |
| Pregnancy Order | Live Birth | Spontaneous Abortion | Induced Abortion | Total |
| --- | --- | --- | --- | --- |
| First | 26 | 4 | 84 | 114 |
| Second | 22 | 5 | 27 | 54 |
| Third | 16 | 3 | 17 | 36 |
| Fourth | 7 | 4 | 11 | 22 |
| Fifth | 7 | 2 | 5 | 14 |
| Sixth and higher orders | 9 | 2 | 10 | 21 |
| | 87 | 20 | 154 | 261 |

Note: N = 114.

## Motivation for Volunteering for This Study

The women were not asked directly why they decided to participate in the study, but the reasons of many were clearly revealed in the interviews and questionnaire comments. Twenty-eight seemed to be participating primarily as a favor to the person who asked them to: in most of these cases the referring person was an abortionist or a physician who had given her sympathetic care at the time of an abortion. For over 60 percent, however, the motive for volunteering was clearly a concern for others. Many expressed a desire to help other women who might find themselves in the same situation. Some of these said they hoped that this research might be a factor in ending the laws which deny legal treatment to women who want abortions; some thought it might be useful to women who are in the process of seeking abortion to learn what others have done, and a few expressed hope that their experience would serve as a warning to other women to be careful about contraception.

All the women were asked whether their feelings about abortion had changed in any way as a result of their own experience. Fifty-nine spontaneously answered that they had changed by becoming more sympathetic to the needs of other women for help during this difficult experience. One of these said:

> Before I never thought much about it at all. Now that it has happened to me I will never again be silent when there is any chance that I can save others the suffering I went through.

Others said, in answer to the same question:

They [feelings] haven't changed much, although now I'd be more lenient and compassionate. I wish laws were more lenient, so less horror would be attached to an already terrifying experience.

I think abortion is a horrible thing, but I defend to my last breath any women's right to have one any time for any reason she chooses. She *must* have a *choice* about the children she will bear. I will go to any lengths to avoid another one myself. [Emphasis supplied by informant.]

Since my experience, which was quite nerve-racking, I am more than ever anxious and willing to work toward making abortions safe, inexpensive, and legal for everyone and anyone.

Twenty-one of the women expressed their concern for other women in terms of prevention of pregnancy, and tended to change their behavior, aside from participation in this study, by being more open and frank about birth control in talking with others. Sixty-one women expressed their concern in terms of working toward changing the laws, so that legal abortions will be available for all women who feel they need them: it will be recalled that many of these women were recruited through abortion-law reform groups. In the meantime, while unwanted pregnancies are conceived and the laws do not permit hospital abortions for most women, sixty-nine of these women say that they are prepared to go out of their way to help another woman, even a stranger, arrange for an illegal abortion. Many of these women had a difficult time arranging their own abortions, and many received bad care and suffered aftereffects. Nevertheless, the response to this experience has not been regret of the decision to have an abortion[1] or a wish to discourage others from terminating unwanted pregnancies. The women who went to the trouble to contribute to this study are anxious to change the situation which caused them difficulty, that is, the present illegality of abortion and the difficulty of obtaining reliable information about it. Volunteering for this study was one expression of that concern.

[1]Only one woman in the study group expressed regret that she had had an abortion rather than continuing the pregnancy.

# 4

## *The Unwanted Conception and the Decision to Seek Abortion*

Despite individual differences, all women who deliberately terminate a pregnancy pass through the same set of experiences. At the time the pregnancy occurs, each has some special reasons for not wanting this particular pregnancy. At some point after conception, the pregnancy is diagnosed or noticed or realized. There is usually a period of nervous hope that the suspected pregnancy will turn out not to be real. At some point, women start acting on the assumption that the pregnancy is real: they tell someone of their fears, start considering the alternatives open to them, and may have a pregnancy test made. Decisions must be made, information and money must be located, and concrete arrangements for the abortion must be made. When the abortion has been performed, the crisis is passed for some women and normal life is resumed. Others have physical complications and must undergo another set of medical examinations and treatment. All face some problems of assimilating the abortion experience and readjusting to relationships which may have changed in the process of having an abortion. For some women, the whole experience is a nightmare of guilt, anxiety, and suffering. Others go through it with little difficulty and no physical ill effects.

The first phase of the experience includes the events up to and including the decision to seek abortion. In this chapter, the women's accounts of the circumstances of conception, the recognition of pregnancy, the decision-making process, and their reasons for rejecting the pregnancy are described. The tasks of this phase of the abortion experience are fairly simple and yet many report that this was the worst part of the experience. When asked the first thing they did when they suspected pregnancy, some of the women said, "went into panic," "thought of killing myself," and "had a crying jag." Others said:

> I was absolutely numb. I stayed home from work and slept for several days. I counted the time backward and forward and hoped I was wrong. I couldn't tell anyone and I couldn't do anything, and I've never been so miserable in my life.

> Outwardly I was calm—I went to my doctor and had a pregnancy test made and I told my boyfriend and my roommate and we made lots of jokes about it. Inside I was just sick. I felt I had lost everything I ever wanted.

> For the first couple of weeks I couldn't think about it. I got up early every day and worked like a dog and fell into bed exhausted at night. Every weekend I went skiing and did all the most dangerous things I could think of. Finally I started crying at home and my roommate came in and I told her.

## The Sexual Relationship in Which Conception Occurred

Nineteen of the women in the study group were married at the time the conception occurred, and all of these conceived with their husbands rather than in an extramarital affair. Two women were not married, but were living with the men with whom they conceived, and eleven were engaged to be married and conceived with their fiancés. The largest group, fifty-nine women, conceived with a "serious boyfriend," a man with whom they had a stable and loving relationship, even if they had only vague plans or no plans for marriage. For example, one of the women described her relationship:

> We had been going together since our last year in high school, even though we went to different schools. I guess we always thought

we would get married someday, but first we both wanted to finish college.

An older woman described her relationship with the man involved in the pregnancy by saying:

> I hadn't gone out at all for the first year after the divorce, until I met him. We work in the same hospital and as it turns out we know a lot of the same people. I really like him a lot—he is a fine person—but I have my children to think of, and I guess neither of us was really interested in marriage.

Although most of the relationships were exclusive, four of these fifty-nine women mentioned another man with whom they had sexual relations around the time the conception occurred, even though they felt fairly sure that their boyfriends were responsible for the pregnancies. Most of these fifty-nine women were single at the time; a few were separated or divorced from their previous husbands.

Fifteen women referred to the men involved as "close friends," meaning they had a fairly stable relationship but no sense of being in love with each other. A twenty-year-old woman who conceived during her first sexual experience said:

> I wasn't in love with him—I've never been in love with anyone. I knew that he had his own problems even more than I had. We went around together all the time and we told each other our troubles. It was crazy of us to sleep together, but we did.

Another explained:

> We had dated casually over the past year, maybe every couple of weeks we would go out. I thought he was nice enough but nothing special. We both were interested in others.

Eight women conceived as a result of casual intercourse with men they hardly knew.

The vast majority of women (106) had no doubt about who was responsible for the pregnancy, because they were only having intercourse with one man. Four women said they had been having relations with two or more men during the month conception occurred and an additional four women, mentioned above, said they had no doubt, but were scored as doubtful because they mentioned another sexual partner in the course of the interview or questionnaire.

Although most of the relationships with the men involved were stable and exclusive, in most cases the man was not the woman's first sexual partner. Only thirty-two women reported that the man responsible for the pregnancy was the first man with whom they had ever had sexual intercourse: most of these were either married to the man or were near the beginning of their sexual life. Although the women were not asked specifically how many different sexual partners they had ever had, the impression given in interviews and questionnaires where it was discussed spontaneously is that the unmarried women tended to have had relatively few sexual relationships, on the order of two to four, usually lasting from several months to several years. Most took their love affairs seriously, and were not promiscuous.

Almost a quarter of the women conceived within the first three months of the sexual relationship and almost 70 percent conceived within the first year. Only twelve women had known the man involved for less than three months when conception occurred, as opposed to having sexual relations with him. This number of course includes the eight women who conceived as a result of a casual encounter. Most of the couples, then, had some basis for cooperation through the difficulties of arranging an abortion.

## Contraceptive Practice

Most of these women were concerned about the possibility of pregnancy before it occurred, and were making some attempt to use contraception. Forty had obtained effective birth-control methods from a physician or birth-control clinic prior to the pregnancy. Six of these forty had a prescription for steroid pills but did not take them regularly, and thirty-four had diaphragms and instructions on how to use them. Twenty-five of these thirty-four claim to have had a genuine method failure, where they conscientiously used a diaphragm but became pregnant anyway. These twenty-five women have a basis for self-righteousness that others cannot claim, and indeed some of these women went to the doctor who prescribed and fitted the diaphragm to demand that he perform an abortion to correct the contraceptive failure. Of these, only a few obtained any help from the doctor on the basis of this complaint.

Most of the young single women, however, had never seen a doctor for contraceptive advice and were depending on nonprescription methods like condoms, douches, or foam, or on "natural" methods like rhythm or withdrawal. About a quarter of the women left contraceptive concern to the man, who used condoms, withdrawal, or a combination of the two. Twenty-three of the couples were not using any form of contraception at any time during their relations: many of these women preferred to call their behavior "taking a chance."

Most of the women blame themselves or the man involved for letting the pregnancy occur: twenty-eight report that they did not use any method during the month of conception, forty remembered that they skipped using their regular method once or more during the month, and thirteen went through the motions of contraception but used it carelessly. The most common form of carelessness was to use a diaphragm without bothering with the spermicidal cream or jelly which is supposed to be used with it. Two women douched regularly but knew that it is an ineffective method, and three used a diaphragm or condom which was defective. These women recognized that they had no one to blame but themselves for the pregnancy, which, however, did not always rob them of their sense of humor. One woman, for instance, wrote "coitus interruptus" on the questionnaire form in answer to the question, "If you were using contraception at that time, what kind or method were you using?" After the next question, "How do you think the pregnancy occurred?" she wrote, "We found out that big words don't prevent pregnancy."

Three of the women who were not using any form of contraception conceived by incomplete intercourse, as a result of "heavy petting" with their boyfriends. Two of these women considered themselves virgins at the time the pregnancy occurred, and the third had experienced complete intercourse before, but says she did not at the time the conception occurred. These women were somewhat defensive about this claim, not expecting to be believed but nevertheless insisting that it was true. Schofield,[1] in a recent study of the sexual behavior of British teenagers, found that very fine distinctions between "making out" and sexual intercourse were maintained among many of the young people, as Kinsey found earlier,[2] although neither study found any pregnancies as a result of sexual contact just short of complete intercourse. These three women had special difficulties with arranging their abortions, because they did not recognize the pregnancy until after the second month.

[1]See Michael Schofield, *The Sexual Behavior of Young People* (London: Longmans, Green & Co. Ltd., 1965).

[2]Alfred Kinsey *et al.*, *Sexual Behavior in the Human Female* (Philadelphia: W. B. Saunders Co., 1953), pp. 282-330.

## Recognition of Pregnancy

Over 85 percent of these women started to worry about the possibility of pregnancy within two weeks of the time their first menstrual period was missed, which is to say, in the first month of pregnancy. Fourteen of these started to worry at the time of conception, because they knew that they had been careless about contraception.

The first sign of pregnancy is usually the absence of the menstrual period, but menstrual periods are irregular often enough for unknown reasons that a delay in the appearance of the period cannot be accepted as a sure sign of pregnancy. Many of these women had had pregnancy "scares" before, when a period appeared after a few days or weeks of worry. In the early period of concern, therefore, many women defined their problem as "bringing on the period" rather than abortion of an actual pregnancy.

Attempts to bring on the period by home remedies, drugs, exercise, and other ineffective means were common in the early stage of pregnancy, even in this highly educated and generally sophisticated group. Over half the women tried one or more of the following methods: thirty-two took hot or cold baths or a combination of the two; twenty-five tried unusual exercise or exertion, like horseback riding, running up and down stairs, or skiing; and twenty-eight took some kind of drug or home remedy. In the last category, they mentioned castor oil, quinine, laxatives, and pills of unknown composition that they got through friends for the purpose. A number of these women felt ill for a few days as a result of their pill-taking, but none accomplished abortion by any of these means.

Another large group, thirty-one, went to a physician in the early stages of pregnancy and obtained an injection of the hormone progesterone, rather than a pregnancy test or at the same time as the pregnancy test. The status of this activity is somewhat different than the entirely home-style methods of baths, exercise, and drugs. Some of the women actually thought that the injection was an abortion, and were considerably disappointed when it did not "work." The physicians who gave these shots were told in most cases that pregnancy was feared and that the patient was upset about it. Apparently these physicians felt that there was a good chance that the woman was not pregnant, and that if she were not, she should be reassured as soon as possible. Most of these physicians were described as sympathetic, and many of the women who obtained progesterone went back to the same doctor for advice when the menstrual period did not appear.

These activities were not effective in ending their concern about being pregnant. On the contrary, these attempts appear to play a role in defining the pregnancy as real, and increasing the determination to have it terminated. A number of the women felt that they had committed themselves to abortion by trying to end the pregnancy in such ineffective ways. Many feared that if they did not go through with the abortion after these attempts they would have a deformed child, although in most cases this is probably completely untrue. If, however, these women had not really been pregnant, or had been among those who, for chance reasons alone, have spontaneous abortions during the first month of pregnancy,[3] they would have believed that they had caused an abortion by their activities. Newman has collected many instances of belief in the efficacy of such methods, and has analyzed them as an instance of "folk medicine."[4]

### Methods of Abortion Considered and Attempted

In an attempt to learn about the kinds of methods the women had in mind during the early stages of their pregnancy, a list of methods was presented with the warning that they differ considerably in safety and effectiveness, to see how many knew of and had attempted to use the various methods. Table 10 presents the answers the women gave to this question. Unfortunately "attempting" to use a method may include going through the motions and actually succeeding in inducing abortion by this means or merely asking around to see if help in using this method would be available. The methods which were actually used to cause abortion are specified in chapter 6.

### Confirming the Pregnancy and Consulting a Doctor

About half the women went to a doctor as the first thing they did about the possibility of pregnancy. All but nine eventually reduced the ambiguity of the pregnancy by obtaining confirmation through a physician's examination or through a pregnancy test.

Seventy-eight of the women went to a doctor in private practice

[3]Estimates of the frequency of spontaneous abortion range from one in ten pregnancies to one in four. One in ten is probably a realistic estimate for spontaneous abortion during the first six weeks of pregnancy for a relatively young population like the study group. See Mindel C. Sheps, "Pregnancy Wastage as a Factor in the Analysis of Fertility Data," *Demography* 1 (1964) : 111-18.

[4]Lucile Newman, "Abortion as Folk Medicine," *California Health*, October–November 1965, pp. 75-79.

TABLE 10

METHODS OF ABORTION CONSIDERED AND ATTEMPTED

| Methods | Attempted | Considered | Heard of | Not Heard of |
|---|---|---|---|---|
| Progesterone | 31 | 9 | 20 | 54 |
| Unusual exercise or exertion | 25 | 9 | 58 | 22 |
| Hot or cold baths | 32 | 3 | 51 | 28 |
| Catheter method | 13 | 8 | 63 | 30 |
| Drugs | 28 | 10 | 52 | 24 |
| Hospital abortion | 13 | 14 | 61 | 26 |
| Illegal operation | 99 | 3 | 9 | 3 |
| Other: douche | 6 | 1 | 10 | 97 |

Note: N = 114.

to have a diagnosis made. Most of these had a pelvic examination as well as having a pregnancy test made. Forty-four of these seventy-eight went to someone they considered their regular doctor, that is a doctor whom they had seen at least once before. Seventeen went to a doctor recommended by someone else, and another seventeen went to a doctor selected at random from the telephone book or from his convenient location.

Sixty-three of the seventy-eight women who went to a physician in private practice told him that the pregnancy was unwanted and that abortion was being considered. Of these, six doctors eventually arranged a legal abortion for the woman, and nine more gave the address of an abortionist believed to be competent. A large group of these doctors, twenty-one, were accepting of the woman's decision and sympathetic to her concerns, but did not offer any concrete help in arranging the abortion. Many of these did, however, offer general advice about avoiding dangerous abortionists, and invited the woman to come back after it was over for a check-up. All together, thirty-nine of the sixty-six doctors told of the problem were generally accepting and supportive. Twenty-seven doctors who were told were carefully neutral or disapproving: many of these warned the woman of the dangers of abortion, both physical and psychological, and advised her not to have an abortion performed. Several offered to deliver the baby at no cost to the woman, and to help in making arrangements for a suitable adoptive home for the child if the woman wished. Eight of the women described the doctor's behavior as nervous when he learned that she was considering abortion. These women felt that the doctor was more concerned about possible dangers to himself than with danger to the patient. Several of these women interpreted this attitude to mean that the doctor had already been in trouble over abortion, and did not want to take any more risks. There is little reason, however, for accepting this interpretation as correct. Seven women in this group described the doctor's behavior as rude, bullying, or insulting: several were extremely upset at the way they had been treated, describing the experience of having the pregnancy confirmed as one of the most painful aspects of their experience.

An additional fifteen of the women who went to a physician in private practice did not tell the doctor that the pregnancy was unwanted. None of these doctors offered any help with abortion.

Some women avoided the possible embarrassment of consulting a doctor by having a pregnancy test made through other channels. Nine women took a urine specimen directly to a laboratory or a drugstore,[5] two had a friend who happened to be qualified to make a test, and twelve used the relative anonymity of a local hospital or clinic to have a test made, to avoid meeting a doctor who might take a personal interest in the fact of the pregnancy. Some of these women used false names and addresses, and most did not tell the person who made the test or gave them the results that the pregnancy was unwanted or that abortion was being considered.

### Consulting the Man Involved in the Pregnancy and Reasons for Terminating the Pregnancy

The reasons for wanting to terminate the pregnancy are closely related to the kind of relationship the woman had to the man involved in the pregnancy, and it is convenient to consider them together.

#### Reasons of Single Women

Only two of the sixty-five single women wanted to get married to the man involved and have the baby. In one of these cases the man felt unready to take on the responsibilities and refused to marry her at that time. In the other case the young couple wanted to get married, but told their parents of the situation first. The two sets of parents got together and talked it over with the couple, and finally insisted on abortion instead. The parents thought the couple were too young to take on the responsibilities of marriage and raising a child.

[5]Taking a urine specimen directly to a testing laboratory to get the results in an impersonal manner is not possible in some states, where laboratories are only permitted to release the results of the test to a licensed physician.

Forty-three other single women came to a similar conclusion themselves. Twenty-seven said they did not want to get married, twelve said they did not want to have a child, several said they were too young, and one spoke of things she still had to do before she would be ready to settle down and have a child. All these women were describing aspects of the same group of reasons, the central elements of which are a sense of the overwhelming responsibilities incurred by having a child and the woman's unreadiness to accept those responsibilities without a great deal of resentment. In most cases, the woman told her boyfriend of the pregnancy and they talked it over before making plans for an abortion. In four cases the boyfriend was strongly opposed to abortion, preferring to get married and have the child instead, and two more women anticipated the man's reaction and did not tell him of the pregnancy. One of these women said:

> He took the idiotic position that we should just go ahead and have the baby and somehow we would all live happily ever after—that people automatically become good parents when they have a baby. Sure, that's why there aren't any screwed-up people in the world, right?

Others expressed it:

> I felt I had to find out who I am before I could take care of another person.

and,

> You have to give so much to a baby—I just wasn't sure what, if anything, I had to give.

Most of the women who conceived with a "regular boyfriend" or in a "love relationship" thought only in terms of marrying the man or having an abortion. It was not clear to what extent the men involved would have been willing to get married and share the responsibilities of a baby, if these women had felt strongly about trying to do so.

The single women who conceived with someone they described as "just a friend" or in a casual sexual relationship thought more in terms of raising the child as illegitimate or giving it up for adoption. These women expressed their reasons for seeking abortion in terms of the handicaps that they would be imposing on the unborn child if they had it. Two women said that they considered it immoral to have a child without being able to provide for its welfare, and one said she could not bear to think of giving a child of her own up for adoption. Seven more women gave as their reason that they were not willing to go through pregnancy and birth to bear a child whose father they did not love. Six of the men who were described as friends or casual acquaintances were not told of the pregnancy, and eleven more were told but took no part in making the decision about what to do.

*Reasons of Women Who Were Engaged or Cohabiting*

Thirteen of the women were engaged to be married or were living with the man involved in the pregnancy at the time it occurred. These women were more confident about their marital future than the single women, but many were equally unsure about their ability to accept the responsibilities of a child.

In one case the woman would have accepted the pregnancy but her fiancé insisted on terminating it. In another case the woman changed her mind about marrying the man soon after conception occurred: she decided that she had misjudged him completely and that to go ahead with the marriage because of an accidental pregnancy would be a serious mistake. She broke her engagement to the man about the same time she received confirmation of the pregnancy, and never told him of it. In other cases, the reasons were less dramatic but equally compelling to the woman involved. Three stressed that it would give a bad start to their marriage to have to cope with pregnancy and a baby right away; three wanted time to get adjusted to marriage before having a baby; one said they simply couldn't afford to have a baby; and another said it would mean dropping out of school for both of them and giving up on the plans they had for their life together. Two couples had set a formal date for their wedding and refused to let the pregnancy change their plans. While they spoke in terms of a reservation for the reception hall and invitations already being printed, the reasons went deeper than mere convenience or ceremony: they were not ready to have a child.

In six of the thirteen cases involving women who were engaged or living with the man involved, the woman reported that abortion was a joint decision; in two cases the woman went ahead with abortion against her fiancé's wishes; and in three cases the man knew of the pregnancy but left the decision to the woman. In two of these cases the woman was disappointed at what she considered the irresponsible attitude her fiancé took in leaving the decision completely to her.

*Reasons of Married Women*

The reasons of the nineteen married women can be broken down into a few varieties: the problems that a new child would cause for the family as a whole, problems with the marriage, and problems of the woman herself, especially health considerations.

Three of the women were having marital difficulties when the pregnancy occurred and were considering divorce. Three more couples decided on abortion upon the husband's insistence. One woman was having marital difficulty and did not want to risk letting the marriage get worse, as she did not want to be divorced. She felt that her husband did not like her when she was pregnant, and that the marriage would not stand the strain of another pregnancy. She did not consult her husband, therefore, before getting an abortion. All seven of these women have been divorced since the time of the abortion.

Some other women were not worried about their marriages but felt that having another child would be unfair to the children they already had. One couple felt they could not afford to have another child, and three felt that their children had claims on them which came before those of a new child. These four couples had all the children they wanted and felt they could comfortably take care of. One of these women was still nursing her youngest child at that time, and she felt that he needed all her attention.

Some of the eight reasons classified as related to health considerations are similar. For instance, one woman said:

> I wasn't able to cope with the mental and physical stress of another pregnancy. We already had four children and couldn't go through another yet.

Another of the women with health problems gave as her reason that she gets very sick during pregnancy and would have had to go to bed for four or five months, while her children needed her. Finally, a woman who conceived late in life gave her husband's health as the main reason for terminating the pregnancy:

> My husband had a cardiac condition and I was forty-five. We have a married son with children. I enjoy being a grandmother but we aren't fit parents for a new baby.

*Reasons of Women Who Were Divorced or Separated*

Eight of the seventeen previously married women, divorced and separated, had children living with them at the time of the pregnancy. Seven of these expressed their reason for deciding on abortion in terms of the welfare of these children. Two said that their children needed all the attention they had available to give at that time, four felt it would be unfair to their children suddenly to remarry and have a new baby without giving the children a chance to adjust to the idea. Two women had doubts about the ability of the man involved in the pregnancy to be a good father to the existing children. Another woman was waiting for her divorce proceedings to go to court, after a long and bitter struggle with her previous husband over the divorce. She was sure that if she was noticeably pregnant before the divorce was final her husband would use this as evidence that she was an "unfit mother" and would get the court to take the custody of her child away from her.

Other previously married women felt unable to create the conditions necessary to raise a child. In two cases the woman wasn't free to remarry, in three more cases the man was not free to marry her, and in four cases the woman simply did not want to marry the man involved. Finally, one woman said that the man insisted on abortion, but she did not give the impression that she particularly wanted to marry him. None of these women seemed to have entertained the idea of having the child and giving it up for adoption.

TABLE 11

MAN'S ROLE IN DECISION MAKING, BY TYPE
OF RELATIONSHIP TO MAN INVOLVED IN PREGNANCY

| Man's Role in Decision Making | Husband | Fiancé | Regular Boy-friend | Friend | Casual | Total | Percent |
|---|---|---|---|---|---|---|---|
| Insisted on abortion | 3 | 1 | 1 | 1 | — | 6 | 5% |
| Active part, supportive | 6 | 5 | 23 | 5 | — | 39 | 34% |
| Somewhat less active than woman | 5 | 1 | 13 | — | — | 19 | 17% |
| Passive or took no part in decision | 4 | 3 | 16 | 6 | 5 | 34 | 30% |
| Was strongly opposed | — | 2 | 4 | — | — | 6 | 5% |
| Was not told | — | 1 | 2 | 3 | 3 | 9 | 8% |
| Not ascertained | 1 | — | — | — | — | 1 | 1% |
| Total | 19 | 13 | 59 | 15 | 8 | 114 | 100% |

## Persons Consulted about the Decision

The women were asked to list all the persons with whom they discussed the possibility of pregnancy and what to do about it. The list includes those they talked with before the pregnancy was confirmed, after it was confirmed, and while they were making up their minds what to do. It does not include those who were asked after the decision to seek an abortion had been made. The list includes—if the woman talked to these persons— the man involved in the pregnancy and the doctor who confirmed the pregnancy. Table 12 shows the number of persons consulted in making the decision to have an abortion.

TABLE 12

NUMBER OF PERSONS CONSULTED
BEFORE ABORTION DECISION WAS MADE

| Number Consulted (x) | Frequency | Cumulative Percent Who Asked (x) or Fewer |
|---|---|---|
| None | 2 | 1.7 |
| 1 | 17 | 16.7 |
| 2 | 18 | 32.5 |
| 3 | 24 | 53.5 |
| 4 | 15 | 66.7 |
| 5 | 18 | 82.5 |
| 6 and more | 20 | 100.0 |
| Total | 114 | |

Note: Number consulted $(x \cdot f) = 467$; Median $= 3.0$; Mean $= 4.10$

When asked why particular individuals were consulted during the decision-making phase, the women gave many different answers. These answers can be generally divided into those which refer to the close relationship between the woman and the person consulted (such as, "we are very close," "we have been friends for a long time," and "we have no secrets from each other") and the more practical or goal-oriented reasons which refer to special experiences or knowledge that the other person may have, the need the woman had for help, or practical considerations like the need for a test to confirm the pregnancy.

In table 13 the number of persons who were consulted by the woman in various kinds of relationships to her are listed, with a summary of the reasons why these people were asked (close relationship or practical reasons). Table 13 shows that those most frequently con-

TABLE 13

PERSONS CONSULTED DURING DECISION-MAKING:
NUMBER CONSULTED AND REASON CHOSEN

| Relationship | Number Who Asked at Least One | Total Number Asked | Reason Chosen: Close Relationship | Practical Reasons |
|---|---|---|---|---|
| Relatives | | | | |
| Parents | 23* | 28* | 17 | 11 |
| Brother, sister, cousin | 12 | 12 | 11 | 1 |
| Other relatives | 2 | 4 | 1 | 3 |
| Friends | | | | |
| Girl friends | 57 | 93 | 68 | 25 |
| Male friends | 13 | 15 | 9 | 6 |
| Man involved in pregnancy | 99 | 99 | 76 | 23 |
| His friends | 10 | 10 | 3 | 7 |
| Older friends† | 7 | 7 | 3 | 4 |
| Other friends‡ | 28 | 28 | 2 | 26 |
| Physicians | | | | |
| Personal doctors | 31 | 31 | 1 | 30 |
| Psychiatrists | 7 | 7 | 3 | 4 |
| Previously unknown doctors | 31 | 31 | 0 | 31 |
| Others | | | | |
| Abortion specialists§ | 4 | 4 | 0 | 4 |
| Woman's employer | 1 | 1 | 0 | 1 |
| Acquaintances | 5 | 5 | 0 | 5 |
| Total | N = 114 | 375 | (51.7%) | (48.3%) |

*Five women talked with their parents separately, in cases of divorce or separation.
†"Older friends" were described as such by the informant, usually referring to a person at least five years older.
‡"Other friends" include married couples described as a single unit, and friends whose age and sex were not indicated.
§"Abortion specialists" are people known to have information about abortion, when described as an "expert" rather than as a friend or relative.

sulted are friends of the woman, especially close female friends like "my best friend," "my roommate," or "a close friend," the man who was involved in the pregnancy, and doctors. Note that less than a quarter of the women asked for the advice or opinion of either parent. None consulted a religious counselor, a social worker, or any professional counselor other than psychiatrists and physicians. Only a few consulted doctors because they valued their relationship rather than for the practical help that was needed.

The persons asked for advice are not, of course, a random selection of the acquaintance universe of the women. In order to ask for advice, the women had to be able and willing to discuss the sexual relationship that led to the pregnancy, and the reasons why the pregnancy was unwelcome. Persons who would have been shocked to learn these facts, including the parents of most of the women, were not told of the pregnancy at all. In addition, many of these women had some idea of the attitude toward abortion of those they consulted. There may be a strong tendency to ask only individuals whose advice is likely to correspond with what the woman has already tentatively decided she wants to do. About half the women were fairly determined to have an abortion from the time the pregnancy was first suspected.

Table 14 summarizes the advice given by those consulted during the decision-making phase. The persons listed in the table as advising

TABLE 14

ADVICE GIVEN BY PERSONS CONSULTED DURING DECISION-MAKING

| Relationship | Number Asked in Category | Avoid Abortion | Advice Given: Have an Abortion | No Advice Given |
|---|---|---|---|---|
| Relatives | | | | |
| Parents | 28 | 4 | 18 | 6 |
| Brothers, sisters, cousins | 12 | 0 | 8 | 4 |
| Other relatives | 4 | 1 | 3 | 0 |
| Friends | | | | |
| Girl friends | 93 | 2 | 69 | 22 |
| Male friends | 15 | 1 | 11 | 3 |
| Man involved in pregnancy | 99 | 18 | 76 | 5 |
| His friends | 10 | 2 | 5 | 3 |
| Older friends | 7 | 0 | 6 | 1 |
| Other friends | 28 | 0 | 19 | 9 |
| Physicians | | | | |
| Personal doctors | 31 | 6 | 20 | 5 |
| Psychiatrists | 7 | 0 | 4 | 3 |
| Previously unknown doctors | 31 | 8 | 15 | 8 |
| Others | | | | |
| Abortion specialists | 4 | 0 | 4 | 0 |
| Woman's employer | 1 | 0 | 1 | 0 |
| Acquaintances | 5 | 0 | 4 | 1 |
| | 375 | 42 | 263 | 70 |
| | | (11.2%) | (70.1%) | (18.7%) |

that abortion was probably the best alternative were not necessarily enthusiastic about it: many of these primarily advised the woman on how to avoid the most dangerous abortionists, or advised her to act quickly if the abortion was to be done with maximum safety. What these persons have in common is that they suggested abortion or agreed with the woman's inclination that abortion would be the lesser evil of the available alternatives.

The largest source of those who advised the woman to have the baby and get married, if necessary, is the category of "man involved in the pregnancy." Twelve of these eighteen men eventually came to agree that abortion was a satisfactory alternative, and helped the women to carry out the abortion decision, while six of these men continued to oppose abortion throughout the pregnancy. The other major source of advisers who urged the woman to go through with the pregnancy is physicians. The category of "previously unknown doctors" is the only group in table 14 in which a bare majority either urged the woman to have the baby or declined to give any advice.

More persons declined to give any advice than urged her to go through with the pregnancy. In the case of the twenty-two girl friends who did not give advice, for instance, the reason generally seemed to be that they did not know much about abortion and could not give an opinion on which of the two alternatives, having the baby or having an abortion, would be most harmful to the woman.

Finally, all the women came to the conclusion that they should try to arrange an abortion: if they had come to any other conclusion, they would not appear in this study. About half made their decision on the basis of their own immediate conviction that it would be best; ten women felt they were coerced into the decision, six by the man involved in the pregnancy and four by their parents; and the rest considered other alternatives and discussed the possibilities with others before deciding upon abortion.

For some of these women it is distinctly artificial to try to distinguish the phase during which they made their decision from the phase in which they sought an abortionist. Several protested against this division of events. One woman said:

> The question was never should I get an abortion, but would I be able to find someone safe.

Another put it:

In a situation like mine, there's no choice of what to do. You know you have two months in which to get an abortion. If you can't do it, you are just stuck going through with it and that's all there is to it.

These women felt that it was necessary to have a definite possibility of an abortion available before they could make a decision. Making a decision, for them, was synonomous with searching for an abortionist. The process of that search is described in the next chapter.

## Summary

The striking observations during the first phase of the experience of the study group can be summarized as follows:

1. Many of the women reported having had considerable anxiety and stress when the pregnancy was first suspected.
2. Most had a fairly stable and even loving relationship with the man involved in the pregnancy.
3. Most of the women had no doubt about the identity of the man responsible for the pregnancy.
4. Contraceptive use was frequent in the group, but many used ineffective means or used the method carelessly. Most of the single women had never obtained any medical advice on contraception: many of these considered contraception the man's concern.
5. Over 85 percent of the women recognized the pregnancy during the first month. This observation has important implications for the possible usefulness of the "once a month" combination contraceptive and abortifacient which has been discussed in recent years. On the other hand, the observation that 15 percent of this well educated and generally sophisticated group did not suspect pregnancy during the first month may be discouraging to the developers of such a drug, in that it suggests that even higher proportions of less sophisticated women may not be prepared to respond in time.
6. Many of the women made ineffective gestures toward self-induced abortion by the use of hot and cold baths, extreme exertion, and drugs and home remedies. None injured themselves in these ways, and none believed that they caused abortion. In addition, almost a third obtained one or more injections of progesterone from a physician. Giving a shot of progesterone was interpreted by many

of the women as a sympathetic gesture by the doctor. Many of these confessed their desire for abortion to the doctor, but few of the physicians offered any other concrete help.

7. The great majority of these women confirmed the suspected pregnancy by having a pregnancy test made. Those who went to a physician in private practice tended to tell the doctor that the pregnancy was unwanted, while those who felt strongly about avoiding possible interference from a doctor arranged the pregnancy test in an impersonal way.

8. Most of the women told the man involved in the pregnancy about the pregnancy, and most couples agreed upon abortion as the best course for both of them. In cases of disagreement, there were more cases in which the man tried to get the woman to have the child against her wishes than in which the woman tried to convince the man that she should have the child. In general, the picture presented is one of women quite unambivalently rejecting the pregnancy, without, however, rejecting childbearing or children.

9. Most of the women consulted a few persons beyond the man involved in the pregnancy about the decision to have an abortion. Woman friends were commonly consulted, while parents and professional counselors other than doctors were generally avoided.

10. Most of the persons consulted advised that abortion was the best course of action among those available. Few persons other than the man involved in the pregnancy and doctors advised the woman to go through with the pregnancy. Since most Americans are apparently opposed to abortion in general, one must conclude that the women consciously or unconsciously selected those they told about the pregnancy on the basis of whether the person was likely to support their tentative decision that abortion was the best alternative available.

# 5

## *The Search for an Abortionist*

The realization of the pregnancy, the tasks of having it verified by a test and telling those most closely involved, and finally making the decision of what to do about it were highly stressful for many of the women. Some found themselves exhausted and depressed to the point of apathy when they faced the difficult job of finding a qualified abortionist. One woman described her condition:

> I was so far to the end of my rope at that point that I was numb. And that was a good thing, because I had to go up to people I hardly knew and tell them I was pregnant and ask if they knew of someone who would help me. I could never have done it if I felt like myself.

Some of the women were saved the difficulty and embarrassment of the search by their husbands or boyfriends, and a few had a girl friend, an understanding mother or parents, or an older friend who took over the responsibility. A few women considered that they bore the responsibility alone up to the point when it was clear that abortion would be necessary, when they "broke down" and turned to a

strong person from whom they originally hoped to keep the pregnancy secret, confessed the pregnancy, and allowed that person (in
one case a guardian, in another an aunt, in a third the boy's parents)
to take over the problem. A substantial number relied on their own
abilities and carried out the search themselves, some because they
had no one to take over the responsibility and others because they
preferred to do it themselves.

Two women in the study group did not locate a specialist in induced abortion, but induced the abortion themselves. Two more knew
of an abortionist and went directly to him without consulting anyone
else about where to go. The other 110 women located a previously
unknown abortionist in the course of a search. The purpose of this
section is to describe these searches. To do this, we need a set of
rules for making the descriptions comparable and consistent. These
rules were developed during the course of the first ten interviews,
and were used as guidelines in asking questions, recording the
answers, and tabulating the results, as well as in reporting the study.
These rules are summarized as follows.

### Criterion for Inclusion

The women were asked to describe each of the persons they asked
for help in arranging the abortion, and all the persons they came in
contact with while making their arrangements. They were asked not
to list those whom they only asked for general advice. The criterion
for inclusion or exclusion of a person in the search process is the
informant's account of what happened. Attempting to correct the
women's accounts is a hazardous task, more likely to introduce further
confusion than clarity.

### Units

Each person mentioned as an independent agent is counted as one
unit. In cases where the couple involved in the pregnancy worked together to carry out the search, the man is classified not as someone
who was asked for help but rather as part of the unit doing the
searching. In many cases informants discuss themselves and their
sexual partners as a single unit ("we phoned a friend of ours,")
especially in cases where the couple are married or have a stable relationship. In other cases where the two did not act as partners, the
man is classified like anyone else if he was asked for help and is left

out of the analysis if he was not asked for help. In a few cases, whole families are treated as a single unit by the informant. More frequently, married couples describe their married friends as a single unit.

## Relevant Information per Unit

Each person (or unit) is described in terms of his or her relationship to the informant (such as relative, friend, acquaintance, formal or business relationship) or to the person who links the woman to the person described (such as "a friend of my friend"). For each person named, the informants were asked why they happened to ask that particular person, and what help, if any, the person gave them. The connections between individuals asked in the search can be inferred from the answers to these questions. In general, one can specify whether each person named was asked for help because someone else suggested to the informant that he might be helpful (i.e., a link in a chain of people who were asked) or whether he was asked on the informant's own initiative ("a fresh start"). This person can be classified in turn as (1) refusing to help, or not making any suggestions (a "dead end"); (2) suggesting that she get in touch with another person, or introducing her to another person, or seeing another person in her behalf (extending the chain to another link); or (3) providing an abortion. The second possibility, extending the chain to another link, can provide contact with an abortionist or merely with another person who might be able to help. The third possibility, providing an abortion, can by definition only be done by an abortionist.

## Inclusion of Abortionists

Each search process, with the exception of the few women who induced their own abortions, includes one abortionist whose services were used. Searches can include more than one abortionist if the central persons actually got in touch (in person, in writing, or by telephone) with abortionists whose services were not ultimately used. In many cases the search provided leads to abortionists who were not approached, either because the woman decided against them for some reason or because the abortionist could not be located. These leads are included in the search process as the "help given" by some person, although abortionists not actually approached are not included as nodes in the search network. Incidentally, reputable physicians who performed a legal abortion in a hospital are classified as "abortionists," at the risk of offending some physicians. The term is descriptive and is not intended to be a value judgment.

## Length of Chains

Chains of persons are not traced back any further than was necessary at the time of the search. For instance, person $A$ asks $B$ for help, and $B$ gives the address of an abortionist. $B$ must have obtained that address from someone else at one time. The sources of $B$'s information are not included in $A$'s search, however, if $B$ had the information at the time he or she was asked for it, even if the informant tells us where $B$ got the information originally. If we were tracing the whole history of these chains of information, the chains would necessarily be much longer than those reported here.

## Multiple Suggestions

The notation for recording the persons asked for help and the help they provided is linear, and is not entirely adequate for describing the several different kinds of help possible. Others may offer the names and addresses of several abortionists, of several people who might be able to be of help, or some of both. In general, information is good about the persons actually asked but weak on the numbers and characteristics of those who were suggested as possibly helpful but whom the informant did not approach. In the case of abortionists suggested by others, this ambiguity was clarified by another question.

## Contacts Mentioned after the Abortionist Was Located

In most cases the search process is ended by the location of the first abortionist who meets the woman's requirements. In a few cases, however, the woman obtained contact with the abortionist she eventually used and went on to ask other persons for help after locating him, going back to have the abortion performed later. In these cases, the abortionist used is not the last person mentioned in the search.

To demonstrate how the rules were used to translate actual descriptions of searches into a standardized and comparable frame of reference, a few actual cases and their abstract translation may be helpful.

The first example is an eighteen-year-old college student who was at summer school, away from her usual home and college community, with her boyfriend and several other friends from college when the pregnancy was recognized. While making up her mind what to do, she told her boyfriend, her roommate, and another girl who had come with her to summer school. She described the search process as follows:

> I asked the girl I was staying with, as I knew her brother would probably be able to help. She was a close friend with whom I had been at school. She told her brother, who supplied me with an address of a girl who had had an abortion. I called up the girl, who gave the doctor's address.
>
> My boyfriend also obtained an address from another girl, and went to see the doctor. He was very unwilling.
>
> I wrote to a friend (male) at home who could obtain pills for me. He was unable to do so since the man through whom he could obtain them was away.
>
> I wrote to a girl friend at home who gave me the address of another man, but I was unwilling to resort to this method as I had heard it was dangerous.

She and her boyfriend finally decided to go to the first abortionist she heard of, which required a trip of about five hundred miles. They were charged $650 for a competently performed surgical abortion (D. and C.) and she was satisfied with the treatment she received.

Figure 2 shows a diagram of this search. There were eight persons involved, plus the woman and her boyfriend, who are treated together as the searching unit. There were four "fresh starts" to the search, which provided leads to four abortionists, two of which were not usable because the abortionist was unwilling or not available, and one of which the couple rejected as too dangerous. The abortionists

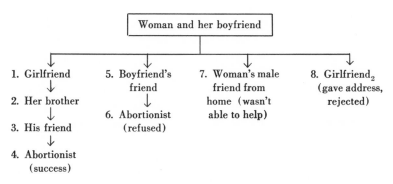

Fɪɢ. 2.   Diagram of a search process—Example 1

in the third and fourth leads are not included in the diagram because they were not actually approached. The chain which led to a completed abortion consists of four links, which can be determined by counting the units other than the couple, or by counting the arrows between the units.

A second example is provided by a woman who got pregnant at the age of twenty by a man she hardly knew, at the time of her first sexual contact with any man. She did not tell him of the pregnancy, in fact she never saw him again after the one occasion when they had intercourse. To terminate the pregnancy, she told only a few persons. She explained what happened:

> I told my two roommates, because they were my closest friends and because my parents would have been shocked and unable to have understood. They had no advice but agreed with my idea of abortion.
>
> I told a close male friend—asked him because of previous conversations (knew he knew of a contact with an abortionist). He gave me the name and number to call and reassurance that previous abortions this man had performed had not resulted in any complications. I also had confidence that our discussion would be confidential.

Four people were told in the process of finding an abortionist, with three fresh starts, two dead ends, and a chain of two links that led to the abortionist used. She did not obtain information about any other abortionists.

The third example is from a girl whose boyfriend was out of the country when the pregnancy was recognized. She described her search as follows:

> I told this girl at school I was worried, and she lent me her car and told me about a doctor in town who was supposed to be sym-

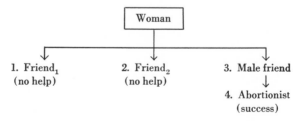

Fig. 3.   Diagram of a search process—Example 2

pathetic. I went to him for a pregnancy test and I had to go back again to get the results, and I asked him what I could do but he said I would have to get married or something. So I didn't push it. When the test was positive I called my girl friend (in another city) and told her I was coming to stay with her and she should try to find out anything she could. When I got there she had found out about two people, one guy in the city from her roommate and one out of town from the mother of a friend of ours. We made an appointment to see the guy in the city and we went there, but it was so depressing that I had an examination and said I would come back but I never did. In the meantime my roommate from college heard about another doctor in the city from her cousin. First we went to the doctor who was out of town. We called up and made an appointment, and went to see him.

This doctor performed the abortion for her, so she never investigated the address given by her college roommate. Nine persons were involved in this search, starting from three fresh starts. The chain which led to the abortionist had three links, three abortionists were located, and two were seen.

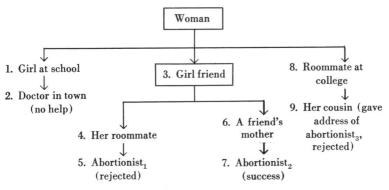

Fig. 4.   Diagram of a search process—Example 3

These examples should make the following tables more comprehensible. Table 15 shows the cross-tabulation of the number of fresh starts the women made with the total number of persons they reached in their search. These two measures are obviously related to one another: it is impossible to make two fresh starts and only reach one person. Note that there are only two cases on the main diagonal of the table, which indicates that it is unusual to use only fresh starts

TABLE 15

TOTAL NUMBER CONSULTED DURING THE SEARCH,
BY NUMBER OF FRESH STARTS PER SEARCH

| Number of Fresh Starts | Number of Persons Consulted | | | | | | | | | Total |
|---|---|---|---|---|---|---|---|---|---|---|
| | 1 | 2 | 3 | 4 | 5 | 6 | 7 | 8 | 9+ | |
| 1 | 1 | 19 | 11 | 5 | 5 | 1 | 0 | 1 | 1 | 44 |
| 2 | | — | 2 | 6 | 1 | 3 | 0 | 2 | 1 | 15 |
| 3 | | | — | 3 | 4 | 4 | 2 | 3 | 0 | 16 |
| 4 | | | | 1 | 4 | 5 | 3 | 2 | 1 | 16 |
| 5 | | | | | — | 4 | 4 | 1 | 2 | 11 |
| 6 | | | | | | — | 0 | 1 | 3 | 4 |
| 7 | | | | | | | — | 2 | 3 | 5 |
| 8 | | | | | | | | — | 3 | 3 |
| Total | 1 | 19 | 13 | 15 | 14 | 17 | 9 | 12 | 14 | 114 |

in conducting a search. In order to be able to do so, one must know an abortionist and be able to reach him without the help of others. In one of these cases the woman had known and been a patient of a doctor known to perform abortions for over twenty years. In the other case, a woman had helped a friend carry out a search six months earlier, and therefore had up-to-date information when she wanted it. She did, however, make three fresh-start approaches to friends for information before deciding that the abortionist she knew was probably as good as any she would find available.

The women who made only one fresh start were obviously successful in reaching an abortionist through the first person they asked. The total number of persons reached by those who asked only one individual as a fresh start represents the length of the successful chain, that is, the first sent them on to another, who sent them to another, and so on, for a total of one to nine steps. The women who made more than one fresh start followed out other chains for various numbers of steps, as well as one successful chain.

As a first step in looking at these searches in more detail, let us see the kinds of persons who were approached as "fresh starts" in the search. The women in the study group, working in partnership with the man involved in the pregnancy in sixty cases, went to a total of 324 people directly for help. The vast majority of these people, 258, were drawn from the close circle of family and friends that surrounds each women. For thirty-six of the fresh starts, the woman reached out beyond her own circle of personal relationships to approach a person she did not have an established relationship with, but whom she had heard of in some context that led her to think he might be sympathetic or helpful: these individuals were described by the women of the study group as friends of friends, relatives of friends, a doctor who had been mentioned as particularly "nice" or permissive about abortion, and, in two cases, abortionists. Only thirty of the 324 fresh starts went to strangers: twelve of these went to doctors selected out of the phone book, by the accident of their position in a clinic or hospital where the women went, or by a convenient office location. Other strangers approached for help were chosen by the accessibility of their occupational role (taxi-drivers, bartenders, hair-dressers, pharmacy clerks), or were impulsively told ("a guy I started drinking with one night," "the manager of the apartment house I was moving into," "I called up this girl I had seen at a party once and said 'you don't know me but . . .' She hung up on me.").

When we compare the number of persons reached as a fresh start with the number of various kinds of persons ever reached in the search we see those to whom the women were sent for help by the "fresh-start" persons. Abortionists are the largest group, not surprisingly, since they are the objects of the search. Other large categories include friends of friends and relatives of friends, persons described as abortion specialists,[1] and doctors recommended by someone else. Table 16 presents the number of persons in each category reached as fresh starts and ever reached in the search.

Each of the fresh starts can be classified as (1) a dead end, in cases where the person asked has no suggestions to make about how an abortion could be arranged, or refuses to make any suggestions, whether sadly or indignantly; (2) a success, in cases where the person asked provides a contact with an abortionist, who in turn agrees to perform the operation; or (3) a step in a longer chain of requests which ultimately ends in a dead end or a success. For all but two of these women, one of the fresh starts started a chain that led to a success, that is, a contact with an abortionist who finally performed the abortion. The length of these chains ranges from one, for the two

[1]The term "abortion specialist" was not used by the women in the study group. It has been coined to cover the fairly commonly described phenomenon of a person who makes a special point of being informed about available abortion facilities, and puts this knowledge at the disposal of people seeking abortion.

TABLE 16

KINDS OF PEOPLE ASKED FOR HELP DURING SEARCH

| Kinds of People Asked for Help | N Consulted as a Fresh Start in Search | Total N Who Were Reached in Searches | N Who Asked at Least One Person in Category |
|---|---|---|---|
| Relatives | | | |
| Mother or both parents | 14 | 15 | 15 |
| Sister, brother, or cousin | 6 | 8 | 8 |
| Other relatives | 4 | 4 | 4 |
| Friends | | | |
| Girl friends (peers) | 102 | 103 | 54 |
| Male friends (peers) | 22 | 26 | 23 |
| Older friends | 8 | 8 | 8 |
| Other friends (couples, etc.) | 27 | 29 | 20 |
| Relative of a friend, friend of a friend | 22 | 120 | 72 |
| Man involved in pregnancy | 45 | 45 | 45 |
| Doctors | | | |
| Woman's own physician | 26 | 27 | 23 |
| Psychiatrists | 4 | 6 | 4 |
| Doctor recommended by someone else | 5 | 29 | 18 |
| Doctor selected by chance | 12 | 15 | 8 |
| Other | | | |
| Abortionists | 2 | 121 | 112 |
| "Abortion specialists" | 7 | 22 | 18 |
| Acquaintances, met during search | 16 | 40 | 8 |
| Other, miscellaneous | 2 | 40 | 16 |
| Total | 324 | 658 | |

women who could directly contact an abortionist before asking anyone else for help, to seven.[2] Table 17 shows the distribution of the lengths of the chains that led to the abortionists used. Almost half the women reached an abortionist in a chain of two links. These represent situations where a woman or a couple asked someone who in turn sent them directly to an abortionist. Chains of three and more may

[2]The longest successful chain consisted of seven steps from "fresh start" to the abortionist used, although we have seen in table 15 that there are two cases with only one "fresh start" and more than seven persons in the chain. This apparent discrepancy is caused by the slightly different definition of the two chains. In establishing the length of "successful chains," we count only to the abortionist used, even if the woman continued searching after that point.

TABLE 17

LENGTH OF CHAIN THAT LED TO ABORTIONIST USED

| Length of Chain (x) | N | Number of Persons in Successful Chains (x · N) | Cumulative Percent Who Reached Abortionist by Chain of x or Less |
|---|---|---|---|
| 1 | 2 | 2 | 2 |
| 2 | 52 | 104 | 47 |
| 3 | 34 | 102 | 77 |
| 4 | 11 | 44 | 87 |
| 5 | 10 | 50 | 96 |
| 6 | 1 | 6 | 97 |
| 7 | 1 | 7 | 98 |
| Total | 111* | 315 | |

Note: Median = 2.0; Mean = 2.83.
*Three women are omitted in this table: two induced their own abortions, and one successful chain was not adequately described.

include people not personally known to the seekers. Chains with more than two intermediaries between the seeker and the abortionist are rare, probably not because information is any more or less available at some distance from the woman's own acquaintances, but because the chain is likely to be ended rather than go on another step if the person who is asked does not have any information readily at hand.

About one-third of the fresh starts, 112 out of 324, led through a chain of individuals to an abortionist, and 315 of the 658 persons asked for help participated in a successful chain. In addition, some of the others who were asked for help did give the address of an abortionist, which was not used either because the abortionist was not available at the time that the woman tried to reach him or because the abortionist who was used seemed better to the woman—because he charged less, was closer, or had better recommendations.

The length of the successful chains having been established, table 18 shows the characteristics of the fresh-start person in these chains, in comparison with all fresh starts, to show the channels through which the women succeeded in reaching an abortionist.

Table 18 shows that half the women reached the abortionist used by starting with a girl friend or the man involved in the pregnancy. These individuals are not particularly likely to have information on a practicing abortionist, but are often highly motivated to search

TABLE 18

SOURCES OF SUCCESSFUL FRESH STARTS

| Kinds of People | Number of Fresh Starts | Successful Fresh Starts | Percent Successful |
|---|---|---|---|
| Relatives | | | |
| Mother or parents | 14 | 8 | 57 |
| Sister, brother, or cousin | 6 | 4 | 66 |
| Other relatives | 4 | 0 | 0 |
| Friends | | | |
| Girl friends | 102 | 23 | 23 |
| Male friends | 22 | 11 | 50 |
| Older friends | 8 | 4 | 50 |
| Other friends | 27 | 8 | 29 |
| Relative of a friend, friend of a friend | 22 | 1 | 5 |
| Man involved in pregnancy | 45 | 24 | 53 |
| Doctors | | | |
| Personal physician | 26 | 7 | 27 |
| Psychiatrist | 4 | 1 | 25 |
| Doctor recommended by others | 5 | 3 | 60 |
| Doctor selected by chance | 12 | 4 | 33 |
| Other | | | |
| Abortionists | 2 | 2 | 100 |
| "Abortion specialist" | 7 | 2 | 28 |
| Acquaintances, met during search | 16 | 7 | 44 |
| Other | 2 | 2 | 100 |
| Total | 324 | 111 | |

through their acquaintance network for an active lead. Note that the proportion of successful fresh starts among these persons is not particularly high, but that many were asked and they produced successful chains for a large number of the women.

Doctors, on the other hand, probably do have access to more information about practicing abortionists than the ordinary person if they choose to collect it, because of their regular contacts with patients who have had abortions and with other doctors who have such patients. Doctors, however, have less personal motivation to go to some trouble to help a patient, because they usually do not know her well, and because they have more to lose in terms of reputation and professional standing from helping women. Doctors provided fifteen of

the successful fresh starts, six of which led to a legal abortion performed in a hospital. An additional twenty-four doctors participated
in chains where a woman asked a friend or relative who sent her to a
sympathetic doctor. Twenty-three of these doctors gave the address of
an abortionist: these doctors might be chagrined to know that many
of these addresses were not finally used by the seekers. Doctors who
were approached without a recommendation from someone who knew
their attitudes rarely helped. Only thirty-six of the 324 chains ended
in a refusal to help as opposed to inability to do so: twenty-three of
the thirty-six refusals came from doctors. The only substantial source
of complaints of rudeness, insults, or lack of sympathy from persons
consulted during the search was doctors, and this was most often the
woman's own physician as opposed to a strange doctor. As we will see
later, many of the women who participated in this study did not go
back to their regular doctors after the abortion was over.

The ratio of men to women among those asked for help during the
search is almost equal (i.e., 1:1) before adding in physicians and
abortionists, which brings the ratio to about 2.5:1. Women most often
ask other women for help, while their boyfriends or husbands tend to
ask other men; but many exceptions to this observation were found,
where women asked men friends or ex-boyfriends for help, and men
asked ex-girl friends or simply friends who were women.

In general, women of all ages tend to ask persons around the same
age as themselves. When physicians and abortionists are included,
the ratio of older people to people described as roughly the same age
as the woman is about 1:2. When doctors and abortionists are excluded, the ratio is about 1:10, and half the "older people" are one or
both parents of the pregnant woman.

**Results of the Searches**

These searches produced leads to 329 abortionists, according to
the 114 women in the study group. Unfortunately, it is impossible to
ascertain how many different abortionists this number refers to. It
is known that at least twenty of the women obtained leads to the same
abortionist, one of the three who helped in the study, because it is
possible to identify him by a description which does not include a
name: eleven of these women, however, were recruited by him to
participate in the study. There were no other obvious multiple references to a single person.

TABLE 19

NUMBER OF LEADS TO ABORTIONISTS

| Number of Abortionists Heard of (x) | Number of Women (f) | Cumulative Percent Who Heard of x or less | Number of Abortionists (x · f) |
|---|---|---|---|
| None | 1 | 1 | 0 |
| 1 | 46* | 41 | 46 |
| 2 | 16 | 55 | 32 |
| 3 | 26 | 78 | 78 |
| 4 | 11 | 88 | 44 |
| 5 | 4 | 91 | 20 |
| 6 | 4 | 95 | 24† |
| 7 | 1 | 96 | 7† |
| 8 | 1 | 96 | 8† |
| 9 | 1 | 97 | 9† |
| 17 | 1 | 98 | 17† |
| 20 | 1 | 99 | 20† |
| 25 | 1 | 100 | 25† |
| Total | 114 | | 329 |

*Includes two cases in which women did not know how many leads had been obtained.
†Tables 20 to 23 include only up to five leads reported per woman, a total of 270 abortionists.

Table 19 shows the distribution of the number of leads reported by the women. You will note that 91 percent received the address of five or fewer abortionists and more than half only heard of one or two. Those who obtained leads to more than five abortionists usually did so by asking a single person, usually one of those described as an "abortion specialist," who maintained a list by collecting information systematically over a period of months or years. The most extensive list found by anyone in the study group consisted of twenty-five abortionists. As has been noted before, women generally stopped searching when they located a source of an address: some, however, located a number of sources at once.

Many of the abortionists to whom the women obtained leads were not actually available at the time the woman was searching. Other leads were not followed up because the qualifications of the abortionist or the method used did not sound satisfactory to the searchers, or simply because a better-sounding abortionist was located at the same time. Relatively few women actually went to see a practicing abortionist and turned down his services in favor of someone else.

TABLE 20

METHODS BELIEVED USED BY ABORTIONISTS HEARD OF,
BY QUALIFICATIONS OF ABORTIONISTS

| Methods: | Doctor | Nurse | Nonmedical | Total | Percent |
|---|---|---|---|---|---|
| Drug-induced | 20 | 1 | 4 | 25 | 9 |
| Catheter types | 3 | 11 | 11 | 25 | 9 |
| Illegal operation | 207 | 2 | 2 | 211 | 78 |
| Hospital abortions | 9 | 0 | 0 | 9 | 3 |
| Total | 239 | 14 | 17 | 270* | 100 |

*Represents at most five abortionists mentioned per woman.

Most frequently, women took the services of the first abortionist they actually got in touch with, and rejected leads, if at all, before attempting to make contact with the abortionist.

Women were asked to describe the information they gained on each of the first five abortionists they had leads to, in terms of the qualifications they were told he had, the method used, the charge for the abortion, and the source of the recommendation they received, if any. They were also asked whether they had tried to get in touch with this abortionist, and if so, whether they were able to do so. Table 20 presents their answers on the method believed used by the abortionists they heard of and the qualifications they were told the abortionists had. Note that a number of women listed as "abortionists" people who would give drugs to terminate the pregnancy, including a number of legitimate doctors who administered injections of progesterone, even though none of the women believed that drugs caused the termination of their own pregnancies. Women also tended to describe the method used to cause abortion as "an illegal operation," terminology that was suggested in an earlier question related to the methods of abortion they had heard of, in cases where they may have been vague about the method used. It is relatively unlikely, for instance, that the two nurses and the medically untrained people listed as performing "an illegal operation" would attempt to perform a D. and C.[3] This ambiguity can persist because the women did not actually get in touch with these people and try to have an abortion performed. In accord-

[3]The term "illegal operation" was suggested to the women who participated via questionnaire in an earlier question about the methods of abortion they had heard of and attempted using. It was used as synonymous with "D. and C." by many, and was loosely used by some others who seemed to be very vague about the method employed.

ance with the rules for describing the search process, the accounts given by the women have not been "corrected."

The unit of information transmitted about an abortionist usually seems to include the price as well as the supposed qualifications and location of the abortionist. Table 21 presents the amounts of money believed to be necessary to obtain abortions from these leads. While 14 percent did not know the amount expected to be paid, most of the women did have a clear idea of the amount of money required, even for the abortionists they heard of but never approached. Information about the method of abortion used generally seems to be more vague than information about price.

TABLE 21

FEES BELIEVED CHARGED BY ABORTIONISTS HEARD OF,
BY QUALIFICATIONS OF ABORTIONISTS

| Fees Charged | M.D. | Nurse | Non-medical | Total | Cumulative Percent | Percent |
|---|---|---|---|---|---|---|
| $100 or Less* | 35† | 2 | 2 | 39 | 16.8 | |
| To $200 | 18 | 6 | 3 | 27 | 28.5 | |
| To $300 | 29 | 4 | 3 | 36 | 44.0 | |
| To $400 | 23 | 0 | 2 | 25 | 54.8 | |
| To $500 | 41 | 0 | 0 | 41 | 72.4 | |
| To $600 | 31 | 0 | 0 | 31 | 85.8 | 86 |
| To $700 | 8 | 0 | 1 | 9 | 89.7 | |
| To $800 | 10 | 0 | 0 | 10 | 94.0 | |
| To $900 | 0 | 0 | 0 | 0 | 94.0 | |
| To $1,000 plus | 14 | 0 | 0 | 14 | 100.0 | |
| Subtotal | 209 | 12 | 11 | 232 | | |
| Don't know | 30 | 2 | 6 | 38 | | 14 |
| Total | 239 | 14 | 17 | 270 | | 100 |

*Most figures given are in round hundreds of dollars. The median of the category is likely to be at its upper limit rather than at the middle point.

†This figure includes most of the doctors believed to give drug-induced abortions and about twenty references to the same abortionist.

Prices charged by nurses and nonmedical abortionists tend to be lower than those reported to be charged by physicians. The category of $100 and less is inflated by the inclusion of doctors who were thought to be willing to give drugs to cause abortion, and by the twenty leads to the same abortionist, who regularly charged $100.

The women were asked whether they had received an assessment of the abortionist's qualifications for each lead they reported. In slightly more than one-third of the cases, recommendations were obtained from either an ex-patient of the abortionist or a physician, who was presumably qualified to judge without having had personal experience with the abortionist. Note that physicians gave recommendations only to other physicians: some of these refer to legally performed hospital abortions.

TABLE 22

SOURCE OF RECOMMENDATION TO ABORTIONISTS HEARD OF, BY QUALIFICATIONS OF ABORTIONISTS

| Recommendation From | M.D. | Nurse | Non-medical | Total | Percent |
|---|---|---|---|---|---|
| Physician | 40 | 0 | 0 | 40 | 15 |
| Patient who had gone to abortionist | 55 | 3 | 4 | 62 | 23 |
| Secondhand recommendation only | 87 | 8 | 6 | 101 | 37 |
| No positive recommendation or source not ascertained | 57 | 3 | 7 | 67 | 25 |
| Total | 239 | 14 | 17 | 270 | 100 |

These women actually made contact with only somewhat more than half of the abortionists they obtained leads to. Almost a third of the leads were not followed up, because the abortionist was too expensive or too far away, because the recommendation was not good, or simply because the woman concentrated on following up another lead which seemed more satisfactory. About one in four of the leads that were tried proved to be unavailable because the abortionist was out of business, on vacation, and so forth.

All the women were asked their most important reason for going

TABLE 23

OUTCOME OF LEAD TO ABORTIONIST, BY QUALIFICATIONS OF ABORTIONIST

| Outcome | M.D. | Nurse | Non-medical | Total | Percent |
|---|---|---|---|---|---|
| Succeeded in reaching | 133 | 7 | 9 | 149 | 55 |
| Tried but could not reach | 35 | 2 | 0 | 37 | 14 |
| Did not try to reach | 71 | 5 | 8 | 84 | 31 |
| Total | 239 | 14 | 17 | 270 | 100 |

to the abortionist they actually used. Forty-six only obtained a lead to one source of abortion; yet presumably these women could have searched farther afield if the source they located had not been available for some reason. Some women who listed leads to two or more abortionists had no effective choice, as some leads were too vague to act upon or were unavailable at the time of the search. Table 24

### TABLE 24
#### MOST IMPORTANT REASON FOR CHOOSING ABORTIONIST USED

| Reasons | Number |
|---|---|
| No choice—only one located | 38 |
| Trust in recommendation given | 33 |
| Safety of method | 15 |
| Location (near home—9; out of country—2) | 11 |
| Price was reasonable—could afford it | 10 |
| Used anesthesia—other alternatives did not | 2 |
| Reason not ascertained, or question inappropriate | 5 |
| Total | 114 |

presents the reasons the women gave as uppermost in their minds at the time they approached the abortionists they finally used. A third of the women felt they had no choice at all: a few responded angrily to this question, feeling that it was complacent and a bit stupid to ask why they chose a given abortionist when they had so much difficulty finding any abortionist at all. Those who gave a reason other than "no choice" most often spoke of the source of their recommendation. Only eleven were guided by the convenience of the abortionist's location, and only ten stated that price was the major factor in their decision. It appears that information about abortionists is too difficult to obtain to allow any effective "shopping around" for women seeking abortion.

### Summary

The experience of the study group on the search for abortionists, and the results of these searches, can be summarized as follows.

1. The women, acting jointly with the man involved in the pregnancy in slightly more than half the cases, approached between one and thirty-one persons during their searches. The median number consulted was five; the average was 5.8.

2. The searches are described as chains reaching out from the

woman toward abortionists. In most cases, the chains are started by personal requests for help to individuals the woman already knew at the time of the pregnancy. The number of such "fresh starts" ranged from one to nine, with the median at two and the mean at 2.8. The most commonly selected "fresh starts" were women friends.

3. The length of the successful chain, that is, the one which led to the abortionist used, ranged from one, for two women who directly approached a known abortionist, to seven, with the median at two and the mean at 2.8. Family members and physicians tended to be most successful as starting points in a chain, if their help could be obtained. Girl friends and the man involved in the pregnancy provided half of the successful fresh starts, not because they had more information than others, but because so many were asked for help. These people tended to be highly motivated and active in searching out information.

4. The women obtained leads to from zero to twenty-five abortionists, most obtaining leads to only one or a few. Most leads were to doctors rather than nurses or medically untrained persons. Most women had a clear idea of the amount charged by the abortionists they heard of, although in many instances they were vague about the method used.

5. About a third of the women felt they had no choice about the abortionist they went to, and less than a third said they chose their abortionist on the basis of trust in the recommendation they received. Relatively few gave reasons that suggested they were making a comparison between alternatives open to them, and even fewer said price was a major factor in their decision.

*6*

# *The Abortion*

There are numerous small differences in the procedures used to cause abortion. These small differences have been disregarded in order to group the abortions the women actually obtained into five types of generally similar procedures. These types are based on the qualifications of the person who performed the abortion, whether anesthesia was given at the time of abortion, and whether the method was basically mechanical or surgical. Mechanical methods are based on irritation of the uterus by a catheter or catheter-like object or a fluid, followed by removal of the embryo by naturally occurring contractions of the uterus. Surgical abortion is usually done by the D. and C. procedure, which removes the embryo with instruments.[1]

[1] A "D. and C." (dilatation and curettage) operation is a common and fairly simple procedure used in the treatment of uterine infections and irritations as well as abortion. The physician dilates the cervix (the entrance to the uterus) by inserting and removing a series of graduated cone-shaped dilators. When the cervix is sufficiently open, the dilators are removed and a spoon-shaped surgical knife, called a curette, is inserted into the uterus. The curette is used to scrape the lining of the uterus gently, removing any tissue which is

The kinds of experiences encountered with these types of abortion are considerably different from each other, and experiences tend to be generally similar within the types. Each of the types, (1) self-induced abortions, (2) catheter-type abortions, (3) illegal D. and C. operations performed by a physician without anesthesia, (4) the same, with anesthesia given, and (5) legal hospital abortions, are illustrated by the actual experience of some of the women who had them. When only a few women had a type of abortion, each case is reported. In the more common categories, only a few examples will be given.

## Self-induced Abortions

Only two women induced their first abortion themselves. The first was a twenty-five-year-old divorced woman, with five small children. She was working in a factory at that time, while her mother took care of the children during the day. She had known the man involved in the pregnancy for eight months, and they had been having sexual relations for three weeks at the time of conception. When she told him she was pregnant, she said he told her "don't tell me your troubles, I've got enough of my own." She told a girl friend, who suggested only that she have a pregnancy test made. She went to the doctor who had delivered her last child for a pregnancy test and hinted that she wanted an abortion, but he did not offer any help. As a last resort, she asked her mother for help, "hoping that she could come up with some old remedy that might help me." Her mother was not able to give any help. In the eighth week of pregnancy, she bought a catheter at a drugstore and inserted it, keeping it in place until the abortion started. She did not mention how she knew this would be effective: perhaps she assumed that everyone knows it. She had severe pain and considerable bleeding for about two weeks afterward, but she was not hospitalized and did not go to her doctor for treatment. Her comment was:

> I had a very rough go of it and suffered more than I should have because of a fear of going to the doctor.

Since the abortion five years ago, she has remarried and has had

---

attached to it. Curettage is not painful, as there are no nerve endings in the uterus. The dilation of the cervix is painful, however, and anesthesia is commonly given when the operation is performed in a hospital. The operation is usually not particularly dangerous when performed by a skilled physician, but is far too difficult and dangerous to be used by a medically untrained abortionist.

another child. Last year she had another abortion, which she obtained
with the help of her husband from a physician for $600. At the age
of thirty she has had eight pregnancies, and considers herself very
unsuccessful with contraception.

The second woman was twenty-three at the time of conception, and
had been married for six months. She and her husband were both
students at the time. She told her husband of the pregnancy: he did
not agree that abortion was the best thing to do, and he took no part
in arranging the abortion. She approached a friend to ask for help,
and saw three doctors selected by their reputation for being sympathetic. Because she was a young married woman, the first two doctors
were not sympathetic to her desire to terminate the pregnancy. She
said:

> They told me about the joys of motherhood, and led me around
> the mulberry bush for weeks.

When her friend was unable to reach the illegal abortionist she knew
of, and the pregnancy was advanced beyond the three-month time
limit that most illegal abortionists insist upon, this woman went to a
third legitimate doctor recommended by a friend of a friend. This
doctor, according to the informant, was:

> . . . extremely sympathetic to my plight. He advised me on the
> catheter system, telling of all possible dangers, alerting me as to
> how to tell whether or not I was successful, how to call an emer-
> gency ambulance, and what *not* to say to the police should they be-
> come involved.

This advice was given when the pregnancy was four months along.
She used the catheter method to start an abortion, only to be taken
to a private hospital where they managed to "save" the pregnancy
and discharged her. Two weeks later she tried again and dislodged
the pregnancy completely. The bleeding was so profuse that her husband again called an ambulance to take her to the hospital. She remained in the hospital for five days, where she was questioned by
police and hospital authorities on suspicion of deliberate abortion,
but no charges were brought. She felt she was extremely badly treated,
especially by the nurses at the hospital. When she was dismissed from
the hospital, she went back to her college courses the same day.

> Following the hospital . . . I was very weak but was so re-
> lieved that the relief seemed to give me the strength I needed. I

also had considerable depression coupled with wild elation for some time and some nightmares. I attributed much of this to upbringing, but even more to the incredible humiliation and mental agony suffered during the entire affair, under the shadow, as well, of doing a so-called criminal act. The general weakness lasted about two weeks. The emotional aspects remained for a couple of years, although I have *never* been sorry to have rid myself of an unwanted child. [Emphasis supplied by informant.]

This woman did complete her college education the following year, and has since divorced her husband and remarried. She has never had a child, and has never wanted to have one.

## Catheter-type Abortions, Not Self-induced

Ten women in the study group obtained a catheter-type abortion from a person who was definitely not a doctor, and two others were told that the abortionist was a doctor but did not believe it. All of these abortions were performed for money and none of the abortionists were known to the women at the time of conception. Eight of the twelve went to a nonmedical abortionist because it was the only lead they were able to find at the time.

A twenty-three-year-old college student, for example, left her college community and returned to her home in New York when she became pregnant. She asked more than twenty friends in New York for help, but the only addresses they were able to give her were of abortionists who could not be reached at that time. She finally located a friend of a friend who agreed to take her to a nurse he knew of in another city, and in desperation she gratefully accepted. The nurse performed abortions in her own home, where the woman stayed until the abortion was completed, with several other women who were getting abortions from the same nurse. She says the pain was fierce and lasted several days, but she did not need medical care. She paid $100 and said she was fairly satisfied with the treatment she received, as the nurse was a decent person.

Another woman, from California, had gotten married at the time of her first unwanted pregnancy, at seventeen, and was a divorcée with a small child at nineteen when she had her second pregnancy. The man involved in this pregnancy made all the arrangements for the two of them to go to Mexico, again to obtain an abortion from a nurse who took women into her own home. Although she said the abortion was painful, this woman was also "fairly satisfied" by the treatment she received. The cost of this abortion was $450: $200 to the nurse, $200 for transportation for the couple, and $50 for incidental expenses of the trip.

Two of the women who received this kind of abortion had not cooperated in trying to find the best abortionist available, because they did not want to have an abortion at all. In one case, a woman with three children was shocked and hurt to find that her husband insisted on having an abortion when they accidentally conceived. Since she did not want it, she left it to him to find an abortionist, probably hoping that he would be unable to do so. He located a man who called himself a doctor through men he worked with, but the informant believes he was probably a hospital attendant or a male nurse. For $75 he provided an abortion in the woman's own home, which was unpleasant but did not lead to infection. Within a year this couple decided to get a divorce, partly because of the bitterness between them about the abortion, but also because they had been having considerable difficulty on other issues.

In the second case the woman was unmarried at the age of twenty-three, but had been living with her boyfriend since the age of twenty. She expected that they would get married, and welcomed the pregnancy when it occurred. Her boyfriend, however, still did not feel ready for parenthood. Since he wanted an abortion and she did not, she left it up to him to make the arrangements. He got in contact with a friend of his who knew of an abortionist, and paid this friend to take his girl friend to the abortionist and stay with her until it was finished. She says that the woman who performed it was unclean, did not speak English, and was neither friendly nor competent. They paid $75 to the woman, who had to insert the catheter three times before the abortion started. To hasten it, she had the informant sit in a tub of hot water. By the time the abortion was completed, the woman was delirious with fever, but took some antibiotics left over from a previous illness and did not receive medical care, out of fear of going to the doctor. Within six months, this woman and her boyfriend conceived again, and got married during the pregnancy. They are now divorced, and she lives with her four-year-old son, working as a teacher.

Three more women said they agreed with their men that abortion was the best plan but took no part in the search for an abortionist out of shyness or dependency. When the men arranged abortions from unskilled abortionists, these women had no choice but to accept the kind of treatment they received. Two of the three had to go to the hospital for an emergency D. and C. operation when the uterus became infected. These women were all somewhat resentful of their boyfriends afterward.

Three more women, however, received unskilled abortions accidentally, after trying to obtain the best care possible. One woman, for example, got pregnant at nineteen, and overcame her reluctance to tell her mother because she knew that she had access to knowledge about safe abortions. Her mother was upset, but approached a number of her friends and tried to track down the location of the most qualified abortionist available. Several of the leads the mother obtained came to a dead end because the abortionist had changed his address or was temporarily out of business. She finally located a source for an expensive, supposedly highly qualified, doctor. The girl was picked up on a street corner, following telephone arrangements, and paid $650 to the driver of the car, who took her to an expensive motel outside of town. Inside, she was blindfolded, and a man came in who was addressed as "Doctor" by the driver of the car. He inserted a catheter, and the two men left the girl alone. She phoned her mother to come there and stay with her while the abortion was completed. When the abortion had not been naturally completed by the next day, the mother took the girl to a local hospital where a D. and C. was performed at a cost of $250. With the best of intentions and considerable sophistication about how competent abortions are arranged, they ended up paying $900 for a particularly dangerous and frightening experience.

Another woman happened to be living and working in Latin America when an unwanted pregnancy occurred, and found that an abortion by the catheter method was the only kind available to her. Her Latin-American boyfriend sent her to an ignorant midwife in a small town, who used brute force to accomplish the abortion. The woman was mercifully unconscious during most of the abortion, not owing to anesthesia but because she fainted. In the space following the question "Were you satisfied with the treatment you obtained?" she wrote, "I came out alive, and I was too grateful for that to think any more about it."

A third woman received the addresses of two nurses who used the catheter method, and rejected them in favor of a chiropractor who charged considerably more, thinking that he would perform a D. and C. with anesthesia. The technique he used was a hot soap-solution douche, which started severe hemorrhaging within a few hours. The woman was hospitalized and doubted that she would live through it for the first few days.

None of these women, incidentally, informed the police who performed their abortions.

## Illegal D. and C. Operations, without Anesthesia

Forty-two of the women obtained their abortions by a D. and C. operation from a person believed to be a doctor. In most cases they were almost surely correct in believing the abortionist to have been trained as a physician, although some may not have been licensed at the time the abortion was performed, owing to retirement, loss of license, or inability to pass local licensing requirements. Almost all these women contacted the abortionist in a medical office or clinic and most of the abortions were performed in these professional settings. Over 70 percent of the women who obtained this type of treatment were satisfied with the treatment they received, although twelve had some complications and five had to be hospitalized afterward. Since there are so many women in this category, only a few examples will be given.

Representing the women who were hospitalized after the abortion is a thirty-six-year-old divorced woman with three children, who conceived in a love affair with a man she did not want to marry. In the course of asking around for a competent abortionist, this woman went to her obstetrician, whom she knew to be sympathetic about abortion because they had spoken of it before. This doctor gave the woman the name of another doctor, located about three hundred miles away. Without making an appointment, the couple drove to see this doctor on a Saturday morning. They found a shabby office in a poor section of town, and a crowded waiting room with patients of all ages. The doctor, a man over sixty, did not want to perform an abortion, but agreed after a lot of talking by the woman. She returned the same day after office hours, and he performed a D. and C. Since he had dismissed his office assistant, the woman had to help him by holding instruments herself. The doctor was nervous about being caught and the woman felt that she had to reassure him rather than the reverse. The abortion was completed in about forty-five minutes, and they drove back to their own city the same night. Apparently the doctor had not removed all the material of pregnancy, as she had mild cramps and bleeding for several weeks after, until she went to the hospital for a second D. and C., which was routine and uneventful.

Another woman was twenty-two at the time of the pregnancy, was working as a high-school teacher, and was involved in her first love affair. The pregnancy occurred after three months of sexual relations, and the couple decided they were not ready to get married. They asked a number of their friends, the woman's family doctor, and her mother for help. They obtained leads to three abortionists, whom she describes as

> . . . a dirty-fingernailed abortionist who was going on vacation, a gynecologist who refused any help at all, and a woman doctor who had clean conditions and was highly recommended by my family doctor.

They went to the third, who charged them $1,000 and performed the abortion in her office with the assistance of several nurses. The woman was given "a little" anesthesia of a gas type, but says she was "very" conscious during the operation. She characterized the abortionist as a "decent" person, and says she was treated

> . . a little roughly but I don't like being probed with instruments. I think I was a bad patient.

Her recovery was simple and there were no aftereffects.

In general it appears that the doctors who performed abortions for these women do not perform many abortions during the course of a year. Although most were performed in a doctor's office, it was frequently after office hours or on weekends when assistants and other patients had left. Many of the doctors insisted that the woman get up and leave the office immediately after the abortion was finished. Unwillingness to give complete anesthesia seems to be a consequence of lack of facilities for giving it, especially an assistant, and a desire to reduce the possibility of an emergency arising which would require hospitalization of the patient, such as an allergic reaction to anesthesia. The abortionists' fees for this kind of an abortion ranged from $150 to $1,000, most being between $300 and $600. In addition, many of the women had travel expenses. It is interesting that doctors who apparently did very few abortions nevertheless frequently drew their abortion patients from distant places. About a third of the women who went out of the country (to Canada, Mexico, or Puerto Rico) to obtain an abortion received this type.

## Illegal D. and C. Abortions, with Complete Anesthesia

About half the women in the study group were not conscious when the abortion was performed. Forty-eight of the fifty-one who obtained this type of abortion received sodium pentothal by injection immediately before the abortion was started, and a few others reported that they received gas or ether. None reported any pain at the time of the abortion, although reports of some cramps or pain during the days following the abortion came from about half of the women, and complaints of "general weakness" were very common. Only two women in this group required hospitalization afterward.

One woman, for instance, went through a difficult period of realization of the pregnancy and search for an abortionist before locating a doctor who was given excellent recommendations by a friend. She and a girl friend went by bus about 250 miles to a small town, where they were met by an employee of the abortionist. She was considerably frightened by this man, describing him as "a Mafia type." She relaxed somewhat when she arrived at the office and met the doctor, whom she described as a nice old man who was very busy but took time to ask her about herself and explain how the operation would be done. After a preliminary examination and some medication, she and her girl friend went to a local motel and spent the evening watching television. The next morning she returned to the doctor's office, was given sodium pentothal, and woke up a half hour later with her girl friend at her bedside. Her girl friend was getting nervous about being caught at the abortionist's office, and the informant says she felt very well, so they asked to see the doctor. He gave her pills for various contingencies and a friendly pat on the back as they left. She had no difficulty in recovery, and felt she was lucky to have found such a nice doctor.

Another woman reported that after trying without success to locate an abortionist through all the obvious people she could think of, she phoned an old friend from college whom she had no reason to think knew anything about abortion. By chance, a friend of that woman had recently had an abortion in another city, and she was able to obtain the phone number in half an hour. The informant called the number to find she had reached an answering service: she left her number and was phoned back by an employee of the doctor in a few hours. They made an appointment for later that week, and she and her husband drove the five-hundred miles and checked into a motel.

They found that the abortionist was located in an elegant old house, with a wing converted to an office with an operating room. A uniformed nurse met them and took a medical history, and the doctor was described as "rather cold and distant, very professional." He agreed to perform the abortion the next morning, but insisted that she must come alone for her appointment, that her husband could not wait at the office. The woman returned to the motel before noon the next day, feeling very well, to find that her husband had become sick from the nervous strain. They had to remain at the motel an extra day to give him time to recover before he was able to travel. She had no complications.

Many of the women who obtained this type of abortion heard about a clinic in Mexico or Puerto Rico and went there. Most of these women received good care, had no serious complications, and were satisfied. Women who went out of the country without obtaining a good address before they went, however, fared no better than women who stayed home and took the first lead they found. Abortion is not legal in these places, and it is not easy to locate a competent practitioner once there, or to find a source of information that can be trusted. Prices at such clinics range from $250 to $800, and total costs are higher owing to the transportation necessary.

## Legally Performed "Therapeutic Abortions"

One woman in this group received a legal abortion by traveling to Japan where all abortions performed by physicians are legal. She paid $200 for excellent and courteous care from a Japanese physician and his family, with whom she stayed for several days after the abortion until the doctor felt she could travel alone. Her boyfriend was insistent that she go to Japan, rather than use illegal channels within the country. Her American doctor made arrangements with a physician he knew before she went. The major expense of her abortion was the $900 plane fare: her boyfriend wanted to go with her, but the cost was prohibitive. Although she is an independent and sophisticated woman, she felt it took a lot of courage to go to a strange country alone, especially at a time when she was upset by the pregnancy.

Six women obtained legal abortions in United States hospitals. Two of these women differed from others in the study group by having an illness of the kind that the laws permitting therapeutic abortion were intended to cover. The other women who obtained legal abortions were similar to the women who had illegal abortions in their reasons for wanting the operation.

One of the women who obtained a legal abortion had a severe circulatory disease. She had three children, and had required medical care and bed rest during and after one of her previous pregnancies. She started feeling ill within a few days of the time her menstrual period was expected, and her legs and feet became very swollen. Reluctantly she and her husband, who is a physician, gave up the idea of having another child, and sought an abortion from their regular obstetrician. The case was prepared for the local hospital abortion committee, and the advice of two other physicians was obtained. Permission for the abortion was granted after six weeks of nervous suspense. The woman says she was extremely depressed and irritable during this waiting period, partly because she was sick but also because she found it very difficult to hope on the one hand that the committee would hurry up and grant permission to terminate the pregnancy, realizing on the other hand that permission might be refused and she would have to continue the pregnancy and raise a child that she was trying to get rid of. When permission was finally granted and the abortion was performed, she reports that the operation was simple but that she was a nervous wreck. She and her husband were very sure they would not have sought an illegal abortion under any circumstances. Although their abortion was entirely legal, they have kept it a secret from most of their family and friends, fearing that others would say they used special influence to get a favorable decision by the committee, since her husband is a doctor. She plans to return to the hospital for a tubal ligation in the near future, to eliminate the possibility of any future accidental pregnancies, which would almost surely have to be aborted. She says that she and her husband were drawn closer together than ever before by their difficulties. She is quite happy in some ways to be sure that they have entered the stage of life of raising the children they already have with no chance of starting over with a new baby.

Another woman who contributed to this study was committed to a mental hospital at the time of the pregnancy. She reports that she received a therapeutic abortion without requesting it, and that she did nothing about the pregnancy one way or the other. She was angry about the way in which the abortion was handled by the hospital staff, although she was very clear that she did not want to go through with the pregnancy. She took a strong dislike to the physician who performed the abortion, calling him "a brute." This woman later induced the abortion of her second pregnancy herself.

For five of the seven women, however, a hospital abortion was simply a desirable alternative to an illegal abortion. One woman was only eighteen when the pregnancy occurred. When she suspected pregnancy, she told her boyfriend, who wanted to run away to another state and get married. She said she wanted to think about it, and without telling him, went home and told her parents. Her mother took her to their family physician, who confirmed the pregnancy and offered his help in any way legally possible. Her mother called a family conference, including the girl's uncle who was a doctor. Although her brother-in-law had information about an illegal abortionist who was thought to be competent, the physician-uncle was extremely opposed to illegal abortion. The uncle arranged with the family doctor to have a legal abortion performed if the necessary letters from psychiatrists could be obtained. The girl was given appointments with two psychiatrists in the week that followed. Each appointment took about ten minutes: she was not told to say anything in particular to them, and she did not lie about her mental condition. She says now that she was upset, but not particularly depressed and had not considered suicide. Both psychiatrists agreed to write letters after a brief talk. The abortion was performed under hospital conditions, while her friends were told that she had an ovarian tumor which had to be removed. While she was in the hospital, her boyfriend phoned her home and her mother told him he should never see her daughter again. In fact he never did see her again. Her parents would not permit her to return to college after the abortion. She completed college while living at home, and has since married.

Another woman tried almost two months to obtain an abortion. Aside from asking her friends, she went for help to several pharmacies in a city in New Jersey that she had heard was a center for abortion and visited about ten doctors in local offices and hospitals. She obtained, and paid for, eight different pregnancy tests (all positive) which she asked for as her excuse to get in to see these doctors. No doctors offered her any help, and she felt that some of them were rude to her besides. In the beginning of the third month of pregnancy, she located a friend she hadn't seen in some time and asked for help. The friend did not know of any abortionists, but recommended her own physician as a sympathetic and understanding person. This doctor explained to the woman, for the first time, the conditions under which induced abortions are legal. He agreed to perform the abortion in his hospital if she could obtain letters from two psychiatrists. He did not give her any guidance about which psychiatrists could be expected to be sympathetic. Once she understood what was needed, she found it relatively easy to convince two psychiatrists that she was indeed desperate, although she found it difficult to locate two psychiatrists who would see her without a two- or three-week wait. The abortion was performed without any further difficulty, and the hospital costs were paid by her insurance company.

Three other women obtained permission for therapeutic abortions by misrepresenting or exaggerating their condition. Two obtained letters from psychiatrists stating that there was a substantial risk of suicide if the pregnancy was permitted to continue, and one obtained certification that she had suffered German measles during the first month of pregnancy. The letters were obtained with the help and collusion of the woman's personal doctor in each case. These were all married women with good educations and a considerable investment in their careers. One described her experience as follows:

> I went to see my personal physician whom I have known for many years, who advised me on how this best be done. She contacted a gynecologist who was sympathetic to my views and was willing to perform the surgery if I could get two other doctors to sign letters stating this was important to my health. I obtained the letters, one from my family physician and one from my personal doctor. Arrangements were made after I cleared the board reviewing such cases, and my abortion was performed legally, cleanly, respectably and successfully.

### Comparison of the Types of Abortion

With a few examples to make the types of abortion real, let us go back and look at the stages of the abortion process. Most of the women were in the sixth to eighth week of pregnancy when they first approached the abortionist who eventually terminated the pregnancy, the time of termination ranging from the second to the twentieth week. At the time of the first contact, arrangements for a time and place and the amount of money needed were usually agreed upon. Most appointments for the abortion were made within a week of the first contact: almost a third, in fact, had the abortion performed on the same day the contact was made.

Table 25 presents the information on the length of pregnancy in weeks at the time of termination. In the interviews, it seemed that women as often counted from the time they missed their first period as from the time that conception occurred, about two weeks earlier. The figures they provided are probably somewhat of an underestimation of the length of pregnancy at termination. In any case, the frequency with which women specified even numbers of weeks—six, eight, or ten—rather than odd numbers suggests that they were guessing about the length of pregnancy rather than making an accurate recollection.

TABLE 25

LENGTH OF PREGNANCY IN WEEKS WHEN ABORTION
WAS PERFORMED

| Length of Pregnancy in Weeks (x) | N | Cumulative Percent at Week (x) or Earlier |
|---|---|---|
| 2 | 1 | 0.9 |
| 3 | 1 | 1.8 |
| 4 | 4 | 5.3 |
| 5 | 7 | 11.4 |
| 6 | 20 | 29.0 |
| 7 | 7 | 35.1 |
| 8 | 33 | 64.0 |
| 9 | 5 | 68.4 |
| 10 | 13 | 79.8 |
| 11 | 3 | 82.4 |
| 12 | 8 | 89.5 |
| 14 | 8 | 96.5 |
| 15 | 1 | 97.4 |
| 20 | 2 | 99.1 |
| Not ascertained | 1 | 100.0 |
| Total | 114 | |

Note: Mean = 8.58; Median = 8.0

*Financial Arrangements*

Many, however, still had arrangements to make before the abortion could be performed. The women found out the cost of the abortion at the time of the first contact with the abortionist. Many had a very good idea of what it would cost from the information given by the person who gave the abortionist's address. Forty-eight couples had to borrow money in order to pay the costs involved. Twelve borrowed from a bank or loan company, giving a false reason for the loan, while thirty-six borrowed from friends or relatives, of whom thirty were told the real purpose of the loan.

Even among those who did not need to borrow money, financial transactions were often complicated and time-consuming. The couples had to agree on the division of the costs between themselves, and many had to make a trip to a bank to get the necessary large amounts of cash. Twenty-two of the women paid all the costs themselves, while sixty-four shared the costs with the man involved in the pregnancy or got him to pay all the costs, and fifteen married couples paid out of their common funds. The woman's parents paid all or part of the costs in only eight cases. The fees charged by the abortionists the women actually went to are presented in table 26.

TABLE 26

ABORTIONISTS' FEES PAID

| Amount Charged (x) | Number | Cumulative Percent Paid x or Less |
|---|---|---|
| None | 6 | 5.3 |
| Don't know | 2 | 7.8 |
| $ 20–$100 | 22 | 26.3 |
| 101– 200 | 13 | 37.7 |
| 201– 300 | 16 | 51.8 |
| 301– 400 | 15 | 64.9 |
| 401– 500 | 18 | 80.7 |
| 501– 600 | 12 | 91.2 |
| 601– 700 | 4 | 94.7 |
| 701– 800 | 2 | 96.5 |
| 801– 900 | 0 | 96.5 |
| 901– 1,150 | 4 | 100.0 |
| Total | 114 | |

Note: Mean = $337;  Median = $300

Table 27 provides a comparison of the fees paid for the various types of abortion. Self-induced abortions and legal abortions are most likely to be reasonable in cost. The table suggests that illegal D. and C. operations without anesthesia are likely to be more expensive than those given with anesthesia: this impression is primarily due to the cooperating abortionist who sent a number of patients to the study, who charged each of them $100. If the influence of this one doctor is removed, it appears that the two types of abortion tend to have about the same range of prices.

*Going to the Abortionist*

Less than a third of the women had the abortion performed in the

TABLE 27

ABORTIONISTS' FEES, BY TYPE OF ABORTION

| Amount Paid | Type of Abortion | | | | |
|---|---|---|---|---|---|
| | Self-induced Abortions | Catheter-type Abortions | Illegal D. and C., without Anesthesia | Illegal D. and C., with Anesthesia | Legal Hospital Abortions | Total |
| $ 0–$199 | 2 | 4 | 6 | 18 | 3 | 33 |
| 200– 449 | 0 | 6 | 18 | 14 | 3 | 41 |
| 450– 1,150 | 0 | 2 | 18 | 19 | 1 | 40 |
| Total | 2 | 12 | 42 | 51 | 7 | 114 |

area in which they were living or staying at the time of the search. The majority made substantial trips, by car, bus, airplane, or train, to the area where the abortionist was located.

Most of the abortionists were in large cities: Seventy-seven of the women had their abortion performed in a large city, thirty-two in what they termed a town, and three in a rural area. About half of those who went to a town were referring to a place outside the United States, usually in Mexico near the California border.

Thirty-six of the women got their abortions in their own cities, including the two who induced their own abortions and six of the seven who got legal abortions. Most of those who found an illegal practitioner near their homes were New Yorkers. The other women, including many New Yorkers, traveled: twenty-five went to places within 200 miles of their starting point; twenty-six went 200 to 500 miles; ten went 500 to 750 miles and six went even farther. At the extremes of distance, three women went to Puerto Rico from various locations in the United States, one went from southern California to New York, one went to Japan from Boston, and one went from New York to Switzerland. Twenty-one of the women paid over $100 in addition to abortionists' fees for the costs of transportation for themselves and anyone who accompanied them, and sixteen women reported costs of $25 to $300 for incidental expenses of the trip such as hotel bills. Table 28 presents the final total costs of the abortions, including abortionists' fees, travel costs, incidental expenses of the trip, medication, and costs of aftercare, where necessary.

While the fees charged by doctors who performed illegal D. and C. operations with and without anesthesia were seen to be approximately the same except for the unusual doctor who contributed a number of cases to the "less than $200" category, the women who obtained illegal D. and C. operations with anesthesia traveled farther and paid higher travel costs to get them. Table 29 shows the distance traveled to get the various types of abortions, and table 30 shows that the women who received anesthesia with an illegal D. and C. most frequently paid over $700 for the total costs.

Thirty-five of the women went alone to their appointment with the abortionist: these tended to be the women who either had the abortion performed very close to home or went a very long distance. Those who went far enough that they wanted company for the anxious trip to the abortionist or assistance if necessary on the trip back got someone to go with them: thirty-nine went with their husbands or

TABLE 28

TOTAL COSTS OF ABORTION, INCLUDING ABORTIONISTS' FEES,
TRAVEL COSTS, MEDICATION, AFTER-CARE, AND
INCIDENTAL EXPENSES

| Amount Paid (x) | Number | Cumulative Percent Who Paid x or Less |
|---|---|---|
| None | 5 | 4.4 |
| $ 1–$100 | 8 | 11.4 |
| 101– 200 | 21 | 29.8 |
| 201– 300 | 6 | 35.1 |
| 301– 400 | 18 | 50.9 |
| 401– 500 | 11 | 60.5 |
| 501– 600 | 18 | 76.3 |
| 601– 700 | 10 | 85.1 |
| 701– 800 | 3 | 87.7 |
| 801– 900 | 3 | 90.4 |
| 901– 1,000 | 4 | 93.9 |
| 1,001– 1,100 | 2 | 95.6 |
| 1,101– 1,200 | 1 | 96.5 |
| 1,201– 1,300 | 3 | 99.1 |
| 1,801– 1,900 | 1 | 100.0 |
| Total | 114 | |

Note: Median = $400;  Mean = $488

boyfriends, thirteen with their mothers or both parents, and thirteen with a close girl friend. Nine of the women were accompanied by a person they met in the course of locating the abortionist, who took an interest in them and went along to help out if they could. Two of the abortionists sent an employee to meet the woman at her home and take her to the place where the abortion would be performed.

The thirty-five women who went alone to the abortionist were asked whether anyone knew where they were that day. The point of asking the question was to find out whether it would have been possible for something to go wrong during the abortion, leaving the woman injured, hospitalized, or even dead, with no one to miss her or check up if she did not return when expected. Twenty-five of the thirty-five who went alone said that someone else knew exactly where they were and when they were expected back; eight said that someone else knew that they had gone to have an abortion but either did not know exactly where they went or only knew of a rendezvous place, while two women said that no one other than the abortionist and his employees knew where they were or that they were having abortions. Unfortunately, the two women who were most brutally mistreated and

TABLE 29

DISTANCE TRAVELED TO OBTAIN ABORTION,
BY TYPE OF ABORTION

| Distance Traveled | Type of Abortion | | | | | |
|---|---|---|---|---|---|---|
| | Self-induced Abortions | Catheter-type Abortions | Illegal D. and C., without Anesthesia | Illegal D. and C., with Anesthesia | Legal Hospital Abortions | Total |
| None, within same city or area | 2 | 3 | 15 | 10 | 6 | 36 |
| 50–250 miles | 0 | 6 | 11 | 17 | 0 | 34 |
| More than 250 miles | 0 | 3 | 16 | 24 | 1 | 44 |
| Total | 2 | 12 | 42 | 51 | 7 | 114 |

TABLE 30

TOTAL COSTS OF ABORTION, BY TYPE OF ABORTION

| Total Costs | Type of Abortion | | | | | |
|---|---|---|---|---|---|---|
| | Self-induced Abortions | Catheter-type Abortions | Illegal D. and C., without Anesthesia | Illegal D. and C., with Anesthesia | Legal Hospital Abortions | Total |
| Under $200 | 1 | 4 | 7 | 18 | 4 | 34 |
| $200 to $600 | 1 | 5 | 27 | 18 | 2 | 53 |
| Over $600 | 0 | 3 | 8 | 15 | 1 | 27 |
| Total | 2 | 12 | 42 | 51 | 7 | 114 |

whose lives seemed to be in the greatest danger from the abortions were in the last category mentioned, where no one could have found them if something had gone wrong.

The setting in which the abortion was performed was closely related to the type of abortion obtained. Doctors who worked in what the women called a clinic usually administered anesthesia for the abortion, while those who worked in their own offices more often did not give anesthesia. Twenty-seven of the abortions were performed in private homes, rented apartments, or hotel or motel rooms, and five more were performed in the woman's own home.

The amount of pain experienced during the abortion is also closely related to the type of abortion obtained. It is difficult to know whether the women's assessments of the degree of pain are comparable: no doubt some are more stoical than others. It is unquestionably true that whatever discomfort is felt is more prolonged with the mechanical types of abortion—self-induced and catheter-type—which require the uterus to expel the material of pregnancy by naturally occurring contractions than the surgical types.

Table 33 presents one of the most unexpected findings of this study. All the women were asked "What was your impression of the abortionist? Did he (or she) seem like a pretty unpleasant person or a fairly decent person?" Despite the often high prices they were charged and the sometimes inadequate care they received, women were often grateful and appreciative of the kindnesses the abortionists showed them. Seventy-six of the women had a good opinion of the abortionist as a person: thirty of these spoke in terms of high respect and affection. One woman called the doctor who performed her abortion "a saint on earth" and another referred to her doctor as "one of the finest people I have ever met." Several mentioned that they had sent personal gifts to the abortionist after it was over, and another said she always sends him a Christmas card. Nineteen expressed some dislike of the abortionist, and seventeen reported that the abortionist was definitely an unpleasant sort of person. One of these abortionists was drunk at the time of the abortion, and injured the woman with the surgical instruments, necessitating immediate hospitalization and later surgical repair of the damage. Another made sexual suggestions to the woman while the abortion was being performed, and several others were described as dirty and ignorant. It is certainly not true that all the women were pleased by their contacts with the abortionists they went to. In the absence of

## TABLE 31
### SETTING OF ABORTION, BY TYPE OF ABORTION

| Setting of Abortion | Type of Abortion | | | | | |
|---|---|---|---|---|---|---|
| | Self-induced Abortions | Catheter-type Abortions | Illegal D. and C., without Anesthesia | Illegal D. and C., with Anesthesia | Legal Hospital Abortions | Total |
| Hospital | — | — | — | — | 7 | 7 |
| Clinic | — | — | 3 | 21 | — | 24 |
| Doctor's office | — | — | 32 | 19 | — | 51 |
| Secret location* | — | 10 | 7 | 10 | — | 27 |
| Patient's home | 2 | 2 | 0 | 1 | — | 5 |
| Total | 2 | 12 | 42 | 51 | 7 | 114 |

*"Secret location" refers to all places other than the patient's home where one would not expect medical care to be given. These places are primarily the abortionists' homes, rented apartments, and hotel or motel rooms.

## TABLE 32
### AMOUNT OF PAIN DURING ABORTION, BY TYPE OF ABORTION

| Amount of Pain Reported | Type of Abortion | | | | | |
|---|---|---|---|---|---|---|
| | Self-induced Abortions | Catheter-type Abortions | Illegal D. and C., without Anesthesia | Illegal D. and C., with Anesthesia | Legal Hospital Abortions | Total |
| None (anesthesia given, patient unconscious) | — | — | — | 51 | 7 | 58 |
| Some pain or a little pain (local or no anesthesia) | — | 3 | 21 | — | — | 24 |
| Pain or great pain | 2 | 9 | 21 | — | — | 32 |
| Totals | 2 | 12 | 42 | 51 | 7 | 114 |

## TABLE 33

### IMPRESSION OF ABORTIONIST AS A PERSON, BY TYPE OF ABORTION

| Impression of Abortionist | Type of Abortion | | | | | |
| --- | --- | --- | --- | --- | --- | --- |
| | Self-induced Abortions | Catheter-type Abortions | Illegal D. and C., without Anesthesia | Illegal D. and C., with Anesthesia | Legal Hospital Abortions | Total |
| Good (a fine person, nice, decent) | — | 4 | 27 | 39 | 6 | 76 |
| Some dislike (cold, mercenary, didn't talk to him) | — | 5 | 9 | 5 | — | 19 |
| Bad impression (nasty, rude, bizarre, dangerous) | — | 3 | 6 | 7 | 1 | 17 |
| Inappropriate | 2 | | | | | 2 |
| Totals | 2 | 12 | 42 | 51 | 7 | 114 |

## TABLE 34

### SATISFACTION WITH TREATMENT, BY TYPE OF ABORTION

| Generally Satisfied with Treatment | Type of Abortion | | | | | |
| --- | --- | --- | --- | --- | --- | --- |
| | Self-induced Abortions | Catheter-type Abortions | Illegal D. and C., without Anesthesia | Illegal D. and C., with Anesthesia | Legal Hospital Abortions | Total |
| Yes | 0 | 6 | 30 | 47 | 6 | 89 |
| No | 2 | 6 | 12 | 4 | 1 | 25 |
| Totals | 2 | 12 | 42 | 51 | 7 | 114 |

## TABLE 35

## DEGREE OF AFTERCARE NEEDED, BY TYPE OF ABORTION

| Aftercare Needed | Type of Abortion | | | | | |
|---|---|---|---|---|---|---|
| | Self-induced Abortions | Catheter-type Abortions | Illegal D. and C., without Anesthesia | Illegal D. and C., with Anesthesia | Legal Hospital Abortions | Total |
| None | 0 | 6 | 29 | 45 | 7 | 87 |
| Routine care needed, no crisis | 0 | 0 | 3 | 1 | 0 | 4 |
| Crisis, but no care received, "sweated it out" | 1 | 2 | 3 | 1 | 0 | 7 |
| Crisis, out-patient care obtained | 0 | 0 | 1 | 2 | 0 | 3 |
| Hospitalized for care, D. and C. | 1 | 4 | 5 | 2 | 0 | 12 |
| Totals | 2 | 12 | 41* | 51 | 7 | 113 |

*One observation missing.

effective social control or professional control over the abortionists, however, it is striking how many of the women were relieved to find that they were treated well by a person they respected.

The women were also asked whether they were generally satisfied with the treatment they received. Table 34 shows that the type of abortion they obtained had much to do with their degree of satisfaction.

These judgments are not merely subjective impressions, but are rather closely associated with the frequency and severity of symptoms after the abortion that result from infection ("septic abortion") or other complications of the abortion procedure. All the women were classified on the basis of the aftercare need to cope with complications of the abortion, whether the aftercare was provided by the abortionist or through legitimate medical channels. These kinds of complications are further classified as those which presented a crisis—by severe bleeding, fever, or other strong signs of acute illness—and those which required care (usually antibiotics) but did not present a crisis situation. The eighty-seven women who required no medical attention after the abortion are almost all the same women who reported satisfaction with the treatment they obtained.

## Summary

These general observations can be made on the experience of the women in the study group of having the abortion performed.

1. Most women were six to eight weeks advanced in pregnancy when they reached an abortionist, and most of the abortions were performed within one day to a week of the first contact.
2. Most of the women found the costs of abortion considerable. Illegal practitioners charged between $60 and $1,150, with the mean around $300. Total costs of the abortion, including abortionists' fees, travel, medication, and aftercare exceeded $1,000 in 5 percent of the cases, with the mean between $400 and $500. Almost half the couples found it necessary to borrow money to pay the costs involved.
3. Two-thirds of the women found it necessary to travel outside the city in which they lived to have the abortion performed. Almost a third of the women left the United States to have their abortions, but most of these went to Mexico, Canada, or Puerto Rico and obtained an illegal abortion.
4. Two women out of three were accompanied to the abortionist by

another person. Those who went alone usually notified someone where they were and what they were doing, in case of emergency.

5. The method of abortion used was the prime determinant of the amount of pain suffered during the abortion, the degree of satisfaction the woman expressed with the treatment she received, and the extent of complications and infection following the abortion. Self-induced abortions were found to be least satisfactory, followed by those induced by mechanical means by a nurse or other nonphysician. Abortions performed by physicians were generally satisfactory to the women and produced relatively few complications, most of which were minor. Women expressed more satisfaction with abortions received from doctors who gave anesthesia than from those who did not, and traveled more to reach doctors who gave anesthesia. Women who obtained legal hospital abortions were generally satisfied and had no pain or complications.

6. About 20 percent of the abortions were septic or incomplete, and about 10 percent of the women were hospitalized after their illegal abortion and received a legal D. and C. operation, the same procedure which is used to perform hospital abortions. These operations were legal because the women were no longer pregnant when admitted to the hospital. Seven of the twenty-six women who had complications did not obtain competent medical care because they feared prosecution from a physician or a hospital.

# 7

## Aftereffects of the Abortion and the Return to Normality

After the abortion had been performed, the women still faced the problems of recovery of their physical and emotional well-being, readjustment of their relationship with the man involved in the pregnancy and others who had been involved in the experience, and the problems of coming to terms with the experience, intellectually and emotionally, with whatever modifications of attitudes and behavior that entailed.

### Physical Recovery

All the women were asked whether they had bad effects after the abortion was performed. The women who had abortions performed by the catheter method were usually describing the expulsion of the embryo as well as recovery in this section, while women who had the abortion performed by a D. and C. operation were describing the effects of infection or normal recovery. The categorization of the symptoms as mild, moderate, or severe was done by the women themselves: it is difficult to know whether their judgments of severity are comparable.

TABLE 36

WOMEN'S ASSESSMENT OF PHYSICAL SYMPTOMS

| Physical Symptoms | None | Mild | Moderate | Severe |
|---|---|---|---|---|
| Excessive bleeding | 73 | 8 | 23 | 8 |
| Pain | 61 | 14 | 27 | 10 |
| Fever | 93 | 7 | 9 | 3 |
| Cramps | 61 | 17 | 26 | 8 |
| General weakness | 39 | 12 | 56 | 5 |
| Other: damage to cervix (1) punctured uterus (1), intestinal gas pains (3), backache (3) | | | | |

Note: N = 112, since two women did not complete this section of the questionnaire.

Twelve of the women with the most severe complications were admitted to the hospital for D. and C. operations to remove infection from the uterus. Most of these operations were necessary because the abortion was incomplete and some of the material of pregnancy had been left in the uterus. Two operations involved repair of damage done by incompetent practitioners, in one case a ruptured cervix, and in the other perforation of the uterus. The second of these women said that she nearly died from the infection. It was not clear from her account whether she lost the possibility of future pregnancies as a result of the damage or not. Seven women were treated outside the hospital with antibiotics and seven more probably should have seen a physician because they were severely ill, but stayed away out of fear.

Nevertheless, most of the physical symptoms which appeared after the abortion lasted only a few days. By a month after the abortion, all the women reported that physical symptoms other than "general weakness" had disappeared. General weakness, which might equally well be considered a psychological symptom for some women, disappeared within a few weeks for all but sixteen of those who felt it. The latter reported that it lasted from three weeks to six months.

The incidence of physical symptoms of illness after the abortion is primarily associated with the type of abortion obtained, as discussed above. Within types of abortion, there is no obvious association between the amount charged by the abortionist and either the extent of symptoms or the amount of aftercare required. The second factor which seems to be associated with the frequency and severity of physical symptoms is the duration of the pregnancy at the time it was terminated. Recovery seems to be quicker and easier for women who have the abortion performed before the ninth week of pregnancy.

## Psychological Recovery

Psychological reactions to the experience are more difficult to assess. Feelings of anxiety and depression may be primarily due to the effects of the pregnancy itself, the abortion, involvement in an illegal activity, or reactions to the crisis in the relationship with the man involved. In any case, about 20 percent of the women reported that they had one or more nightmares after the experience, but no one said that nightmares were a severe problem. Four of the women who were interviewed reported nightmares, and they were asked what the dream consisted of: two of these had dreams of being chased and running away, and two had dreams of hurting a child or seeing a hurt child. One woman reported occasional feelings of great regret for having had the abortion, and another woman feared sterility for several years afterward, until her fears were put to rest by the birth of her first child.

TABLE 37

WOMEN'S ASSESSMENT OF PSYCHOLOGICAL SYMPTOMS

| Psychological Symptoms | None | Mild | Moderate | Severe |
|---|---|---|---|---|
| Depression | 61 | 11 | 31 | 9 |
| Nightmares | 89 | 4 | 19 | 0 |
| Other: regret of decision (1); fears of sterility (1) | | | | |

Note: N = 112, since two women did not complete this section of the questionnaire.

Reports of depression were most common, and tended to be reported by the same women who mentioned nightmares. Incidence of depression was found to be associated with the woman's impression of the abortionist as a person, suggesting that women who are given adequate care by a person they respect are less likely to become depressed; with the amount of aftercare required, especially for the women who were hospitalized afterward; and with the deterioration of the relationship with the man involved in the pregnancy. Religious background, self-blame over carelessness with contraception, and the kind of relationship with the man involved in the pregnancy did not seem to be particularly related to the incidence of depression.

The question concerning depression was asked in reference to the period of time just following the abortion. Many women volunteered that they had been far more depressed before the abortion was performed, during the period of making the decision and searching for an abortionist, than they were afterward. In answer to the question whether they experienced depression after the abortion, a number of women wrote "no—relieved" in the space provided.

Eight of the women mentioned that they have received psychotherapy since the abortion and have talked with their psychiatrist or psychologist about the abortion experience. Four of these women had started treatment before the pregnancy occurred. Only one reported that she needed psychotherapy as a direct result of the abortion: she added $1,000 in psychiatrist's fees to the total cost of the abortion she obtained.

## Routine Medical Aftercare

One of the sources of concern to many women, including many who did not have any noticeable ill effects after the abortion, was the possibility that they had been injured in some way without knowing it. Another common concern was the fear of becoming pregnant again by continued use of inadequate contraceptive methods. In order to have a physical check-up and obtain contraceptive advice, many of the women were anxious to consult a regular doctor after the abortion.

Sixty-nine of the women went to doctors and told them that they had had abortions if the doctors did not already know it: nineteen of these women asked only for a physical examination and fifty requested both an examination and contraceptive advice. Nine more women went to doctors for examinations but did not tell them that they had had abortions. Thirty-two of the women either did not care about having a check-up or were afraid that the doctor could recognize an illegal abortion from examination and stayed away.

Forty-four women had gone to their "regular doctors" before the abortion, to ask for a pregnancy test and in some cases for help in arranging an abortion. Fourteen of these women changed doctors after the abortion and most of these said that they would never go back to their regular doctors, either because they had been asked for help and had refused to give any, or because the women feared they would turn them in to the police, tell their parents or shame them in some way. Twenty of the women gained doctors in the course of the abortion proceedings, most of whom had been sympathetic, some of whom had offered help in arranging the abortion, and many of whom had told the women to come back for a checkup after it was over.

## Changes in Contraceptive Use

Before the abortion, many of the women had been using contraceptive methods carelessly or had been using ineffective methods. When sexual relations were resumed after the abortion, most had improved their contraceptive methods and use. Sixty-one of the women started taking pills, twelve got an intrauterine device (the "coil" or "loop"), three joined an experimental program at the Margaret Sanger Clinic in New York, and two had tubal ligations. These seventy-eight women produced five of the twenty-six second abortions, all because they discontinued using their method after some time. Twenty-six women went back to using relatively ineffective methods of contraception, although many changed to a slightly more effective method than they had used before the pregnancy: they produced sixteen of the second abortions. Four of the women who used no method before the pregnancy continued not to use any, and six of the women swore off sexual relations entirely for a while after the abortion and were not prepared with effective contraception when relations were resumed. These ten women produced five of the twenty-six second abortions.

## Changes in the Relationship with the Man Involved in the Pregnancy

The unwanted pregnancy and abortion produced a crisis in the relationship of almost all the couples who went through the experience. It was a time of considerable stress for both the men and the women, according to the women, and a time which required both of them to mobilize their social, emotional, and financial resources to cope with the situation. Under the conditions of crisis, twenty-three of the women reported that their relationship with the man involved improved during the pregnancy and recovery period. For these couples, the joint problems they faced brought them closer together and gave them an opportunity to demonstrate and appreciate the love and understanding they shared. Thirty-nine women said there was no change in their relationship, but four of these revealed considerable resentment toward the man elsewhere in the interview or questionnaire. Fifty of the women reported that the relationship got worse or deteriorated entirely during the approximately three-month period between conception and abortion, while two women had no on-going relationship with the man and never saw him again after conception.

Sixty couples broke off their relationship when the abortion was completed. Only eighteen of the sixty said that the abortion was the only reason for the break-up: the rest of the women felt it would have happened eventually in any case. Most of the women interpreted the break-up as due to basic disagreements or a lack of love which was merely brought to the surface by the problem of the unwanted pregnancy. Some of the couples, as described above, had not basically agreed about the need for abortion: it is striking that in every case where one party insisted upon abortion against the wishes of the other, the couple broke up afterward. A few women described suspicion and resentment building up between them in cases where the man suspected that the pregnancy was conceived deliberately in order to force him into marriage, or felt that the woman was trying to extract an unfair proportion of the necessary money from him or was being extravagant in choosing to go to a more expensive or more distant abortionist rather than using a cheaper lead. The complaints that women made against men were that they did not accept responsibility for making the decision, did not do their share of searching for a competent abortionist, were willing to risk the woman's health in order to save money, or, most commonly, did not give the emotional support the woman felt she needed. Ten of the women reported that they hated the man involved before it was over.

Of the fifty-two couples who stayed together throughout the pregnancy and for some time afterward, ten couples broke up long after the abortion for reasons unconnected with it, thirty have continued their relationship on the same basis as before the abortion, eight have married, and four more have set a wedding date and expect to marry soon.

Among the women who broke off the relationship, twenty-one have married someone else since that time. Seventeen have told their husbands about the abortion experience and four have not.

**Changes in Other Relationships**

Some women gained a new doctor in the course of the abortion experience, and some lost the doctor they had. Many experienced radical changes in their relationship with the man involved in the pregnancy. Aside from these two categories, few women mentioned changes in their relationships to other people who were important to them. One woman who went to her sister for help said that they had become much closer friends since the abortion, and that her sister had finally come to accept her as an adult. Another woman mentioned that one of her close female friends could not accept her decision to have an abortion, first tried to talk her out of it, and, failing that, has never spoken to her again.

Managing the relationship with parents was a source of concern to many of the women. Most of them handled the problem by keeping the experience secret from their parents, which may have had the effect of alienating the family somewhat. Most of these women were already keeping the facts of their sexual activity secret from their parents, either because they felt their parents would be shocked or because they felt their parents would worry about them. The women who had previously discussed their sexual relations with their parents tended to be the same women who told their parents about the unwanted pregnancy and accepted help in arranging the abortion.

Three women who did not have the kind of relationship with their parents that encouraged open discussion of personal problems nevertheless told their parents under the strain of the abortion situation and had reason to regret it. One of these was the eighteen-year-old who had been considering eloping with her boyfriend before she told her parents, who arranged a legal hospital abortion for her. She says her relationship with her parents changed a great deal after that experience. Prior to the pregnancy, her parents had permitted her to make many of her own decisions and had never interfered with her choice of friends. After the abortion, her parents forbade her to return to a residential college and broke off her relationship with the boy involved in the pregnancy. She was kept at home under considerable restriction until she had finished college at a local school and married another man. The second woman was twenty-seven at the time of her pregnancy: her parents were very proud of her for having been an excellent student and for holding a very good job in New York. She found it extremely difficult to decide what to do when she discovered that she was pregnant. The only alternative that she could accept as proper was marriage to the man involved, which was out of the question, as she knew that he had no serious intentions at the time they started their brief affair. In the turmoil of trying to decide what to do, she consulted a kind and sympathetic doctor who strongly urged her to tell her parents and ask for their help. Dutifully, she took a plane to her mid-Western home and told her parents of her difficulty. Her parents were shocked and angry that she expected them to help her. They expressed the same values that had made it so difficult for her to act; that she should not have had sexual relations with a man she could not expect to marry; that illegitimacy and abortion were equally unacceptable; and that whatever she decided to do she should do it quietly and not bring shame on her family. She returned to New York and arranged an abortion without too much difficulty through one of her many sophisticated friends. Over a year after the event, she still had a great deal of difficulty in accepting the fact that she was a woman who had had an abortion. Her greatest regret was that she had forced the problem on her parents and had upset them unnecessarily. She said:

> Why do we have this naive belief that families will be better off if they face the "realities of life"? I knew perfectly well that my parents could not help me, but I wanted to do the right thing and that seemed like it at the time. All they really cared about when it came right down to it was that the neighbors shouldn't find out.

The third woman had gone to Japan and found it possible to make a stopover to see her parents on the return trip at no additional cost. She arrived unexpectedly bearing gifts she had bought in Japan, which naturally mystified her parents. She says she was surprised that they accepted her vague explanation with so few questions. She took her father aside and told him that she had been to Japan to have an abortion. His only comment and request was that she should not tell her mother. She too felt afterward that it had been childish of her to go home and try to win acceptance of what she had done, however indirectly. She said:

> If I had it to do over, I would have forgotten about the money
> and just come back directly. What's the good of making your
> parents happy with a visit if it makes them worry about you?

## Coming to Terms with the Experience

From the time the pregnancy was recognized to the time when
the abortion was completed, the women had a great deal on their
minds—what to do, how to do it, whom to tell, anxiety about
whether abortion would be possible, fear of the operation, of injury,
or of death, emotional involvement in the crisis with the man involved in the pregnancy, and so on. Several of the women mentioned
feeling numb or dazed during the whole procedure. One by one
the concrete tasks before them were met, leaving the ambiguous
problem of assimilating the experience and coming to terms with
the abortion as a part of their lives to be gradually confronted in
the months and even years following their experience.

Relatively few women seemed to be able to accept the abortion
as a part of their life like any other, without taking some kind of
an attitude toward the experience and developing it into an abstract
position. The study group was made up of a number of intelligent
and verbal women. Many of them "made sense" out of their experience, and many said that they had changed their behavior as a
result of this process.

The positions taken might be seen as a continuum between "encapsulation" of the experience, on the one hand, and "politicization"
on the other.

Women who encapsulated their experience tended to break off
all connections with the persons who had been involved in the abortion experience and hoped to keep it a secret in the future. Some
of these women broke off from the man involved in the pregnancy
and hoped never to see him again: other couples stayed together
and kept the fact of the abortion a secret between themselves, in
at least two cases never mentioning it again. Some of these women
were obviously handling their feelings about the experience by
the psychological defense of denial. One woman, for instance, who
recounted her experience briefly and factually without any mention
of how she felt about it, appeared surprised at a question concerning
her reactions. She said:

> I don't actually remember much about that. It seems more like
> I watched the whole thing happening to someone else.

Not all the women who encapsulated their experience were unable
to think about it. Some women who appeared to be very much in
touch with their own feelings and entirely realistic about the situation were primarily motivated to protect their personal or professional reputations. One woman said:

> I've sometimes felt very ashamed of my cowardice when the
> subject came up and people started talking nonsense about it. But
> there is so much prejudice against women in my field of work that
> I just couldn't afford to give people reason to talk and sneer and
> feel superior.

At the other extreme, some women reacted to their own experience by making it the basis of political conviction and action. Some
of the women have taken a defiant and principled place in the
"underground" of abortion, by becoming self-appointed "abortion
specialists" who go out of their way to be available and helpful
to anyone seeking illegal abortion. Some of the women have chosen
instead to express their conviction through the ordinary forms of
legislative reform action by joining lobby groups or public-education
groups, writing to newspapers and congressmen, and so forth. The
two kinds of action are not mutually exclusive: some of the politi-
cally oriented women do both, and some do neither.

No doubt the study group overrepresents women who have taken
a strongly politicized position on abortion after their experience,
and underrepresents the women who encapsulate their experience
and keep silent about it after it is over, as such women are unlikely
to freely volunteer to be a part of such a study. Without placing
too much weight on these orientations, we can see traces of the
effects of some such process on the behavior of the women following
their abortion experience, in the persons they told about the experience, the ones they kept it secret from, and the extent to which
they made themselves available to help others seeking abortion.

## Control of Communication

### Telling Others

After the abortion was completed, there was no practical need
to tell more people about the abortion experience, except for those
doctors who were told in the course of a physical examination. Most

of the women, however, have told substantial numbers of people about their experience since it happened. On the average, more persons were told after it was all over than were told when it occurred. The number who have been told since it happened depends to some extent on the amount of time which has passed since the experience. The women who obtained questionnaires from their abortionists usually had not had time to talk with anyone after it was over, while some women had had a number of years in which to talk with others. One might expect that the numbers specified by women who had their abortion experience a number of years ago may be more inaccurate than those reporting on a recent event, as they have also had more time to forget about telling some persons. Table 38 presents the number of persons told after the abortion, by the number of years which have elapsed.

TABLE 38

NUMBER OF OTHERS TOLD OF THE ABORTION
BY YEARS SINCE THE EXPERIENCE

| Years Since | None | 1–5 | Number Told Since 6–10 | 11–30 | 31–50 | 51 + | Total |
|---|---|---|---|---|---|---|---|
| Less than 1 | 10 | 23 | 4 | 5 | 0 | 0 | 42 |
| 2 | 0 | 3 | 5 | 2 | 0 | 1 | 11 |
| 3 | 0 | 4 | 1 | 3 | 1 | 0 | 9 |
| 4 | 1 | 4 | 1 | 5 | 1 | 3 | 15 |
| More than 4 | 0 | 16 | 3 | 11 | 5 | 2 | 37 |
| Totals | 11 | 50 | 14 | 26 | 7 | 6 | 114 |

The kinds of people with whom the women discussed the abortion after it was over are summarized in table 39. Most of the women talked about it at least with a doctor or a girl friend: most of those who were told about it were girl friends and others seeking abortion. Women who had disliked the abortionist they went to, had been frightened by the experience, and particularly those who had been depressed by the experience tended to tell many friends about it.

*Keeping the Experience Secret*

While the women have told substantial numbers of other persons about their experience, many of them are concerned to keep their experience secret from some others. All the women were asked, "Are there any people that you are particularly anxious should *not* find

TABLE 39

NUMBER OF OTHERS TOLD OF EXPERIENCE,
BY CATEGORIES OF PEOPLE

| | | | | | | Number Told | |
|---|---|---|---|---|---|---|---|
| Kinds of People | None | 1 | 2 | 3 | 4 | 5 + | Not Ascertained | Total |
| Family members | 77 | 18 | 6 | 6 | 1 | 3 | 3 | 114 |
| Doctors | 40 | 36 | 16 | 10 | 6 | 3 | 3 | 114 |
| Girl friends | 46 | 10 | 14 | 12 | 4 | 24 | 4 | 114 |
| Male friends | 85 | 7 | 6 | 1 | 3 | 9 | 3 | 114 |
| Sexual partners | 72 | 23 | 8 | 1 | 3 | 4 | 3 | 114 |
| Others seeking abortion | 55 | 31 | 2 | 4 | 1 | 20 | 1 | 114 |

out about your experience, like your parents, your children, or your employer or family doctor?" Despite the alternatives suggested by the question, a wide range of persons were mentioned in the answers, and many of the women listed a number of different individuals or groups of people.

All the women, therefore, have been classified on the basis of their answers to this question. Twenty-seven women said they wanted to keep the experience a secret from "everyone": some of these women mentioned specific individuals or groups as well. Forty-four are grouped together as primarily concerned that their mothers, fathers, both parents, or whole families should not learn about the experience. Some of these women mentioned others as well, but none said "everyone." Seven are primarily concerned that their own children not find out. This group, plus the eight who mentioned concern about their own children and also mentioned "everyone" or the parental family, includes all the women except one who have children old enough to understand what abortion is. Even the fifty-two-year-old grandmother in the group was concerned about keeping her experience from her children. Twenty-eight of the women were sufficiently concerned about their employers, co-workers, or school authorities to mention them, but all but four were more concerned about other groups. Thirty-two are grouped together because they are not keeping it a secret from anyone, or because they mentioned only specific individuals for idiosyncratic reasons, such as "one of the women at work, who is Catholic and would never understand" and "my best friend, because she and her husband can't have any children."

Table 40 shows all the major groups mentioned in answer to this question, subdivided by the types of people the women are primarily concerned about. Note that sixty-one of the women list their parents or parental family as persons from whom the secret is being kept. This number includes all of those who did not ask their parents for help during the decision-making and search phases of the abortion. Note too that only two women spontaneously mentioned the police or legal authorities, although none told the police about their experience. After the abortion is over the dangers of the illegality of abortion are relatively unimportant, but women continue to be concerned about protecting others who might be shocked or hurt to hear about it, protecting their relationship with some of these persons, especially parents, and protecting their reputations.

Keeping the experience secret is related to the number of persons the women told about their abortion. The women who were keeping their experience secret from "everyone" told an average of 3.7 persons about it after it occurred; those keeping it secret primarily from their parents told an average of about nine others; those primarily concerned about their own children told an average of eleven; and those who were not keeping it secret from anyone or only from a few persons for idiosyncratic reasons told an average of eighteen.

*Helping Others Who Seek Abortion*

The women who told a considerable number, ten or more, about their experience, generally did so in the process of helping others who wanted to terminate a pregnancy, in an attempt to work toward reform of the laws prohibiting abortion, or both. As is seen in table 39, more than half the women discussed their own experience with others seeking abortion. Fifty of the women were asked for the address of the abortionist they went to by others who reached them through a search process, or volunteered their help when they heard of someone who was pregnant and wanted an abortion. Forty of these women gave the address of the abortionist they used, while ten would not give out the address because the abortionist was not available to others or because the woman was treated badly and would not recommend him. Thirty-two of these fifty women who had an opportunity to help someone else gave help in other ways besides giving the address, such as giving other addresses which had been collected during their search, talking with the other

## TABLE 40

### PERSONS FROM WHOM THE ABORTION IS BEING KEPT SECRET, BY THE TYPES OF PEOPLE THE WOMAN IS PRIMARILY CONCERNED ABOUT

| Kinds of People | Types | | | | | N Keeping Secret From at Least One Person in Group |
|---|---|---|---|---|---|---|
| | Everyone | Primarily Concerned about Parents | Primarily Concerned about Own Children | Primarily Concerned about Co-workers | Idiosyncratic Choices Only | |
| Everyone | 27 | — | — | — | — | 27 |
| Mother, father, parents whole family | 17 | 44 | — | — | — | 61 |
| Own children | 5 | 3 | 7 | — | — | 15 |
| Employer, co-workers, school authorities | 9 | 15 | 0 | 4 | — | 28 |
| Husband, boyfriend, current and future | 5 | 1 | 2 | 1 | 3 | 12 |
| Girl friends | 4 | 2 | 1 | 0 | 1 | 8 |
| Male friends | 4 | 1 | 1 | 0 | 1 | 7 |
| Family friends, neighbors | 2 | 3 | 0 | 0 | 1 | 6 |
| People who disapprove, who would be shocked | 3 | 2 | 1 | 1 | 0 | 7 |
| Police, law-enforcement agencies | 0 | 2 | 0 | 0 | 0 | 2 |
| No one | 0 | 0 | 0 | 0 | 26 | — |
| Total | 27 | 44 | 7 | 4 | 32 | 114 |

woman to give her an idea of what to expect, and, in eighteen cases, actually traveling with the other woman when she went to the abortionist, to help in any way she could. Most of these women were helping personal friends, but a few were introduced to someone they had not previously known who needed help, and gave it freely. We see the role of "abortion specialist" in the process of formation.

The need or desire to keep the abortion secret from particular individuals is related to the number of people actually helped, but it is not closely associated with willingness to help others. In answer to the question "Would you go out of your way to help someone you didn't know get an abortion?" 56 percent of those who wanted to keep the abortion a secret from everyone said "yes," as did 88 percent of those who were keeping it a secret from parents or children and 61 percent of those who were not keeping it a secret from anyone or only from certain people. Those who play the largest role in helping others arrange abortion and in working toward changing the laws concerning abortion must have not only a desire and willingness to do so, but also an absence of persons from whom their own experience must be kept a secret.

## The Schedule of Recovery from Effects of the Abortion

Within a few days most of the women had recovered from physical ill effects of the abortion, and within a month almost all had regained their health. Recovery from the anxiety and depression of the experience occurred gradually over the next few months for most of the women, complicated for some by the turmoil of breaking up with the man involved in the pregnancy. Most of the women gave the impression that by six months after the abortion the experience had receded to a minor place in their day-to-day consciousness, replaced by less dramatic but equally important events in their families, their romances, their work, or their studies.

Perhaps the most striking observation that emerges from the experiences of the women who contributed to this study is the absence of long-range consequences of the unwanted pregnancy on their subsequent life, in comparison with the consequences which would necessarily have followed the pregnancy had it not been terminated. The women in the group tended to have fairly high educational achievements prior to their experience with unwanted pregnancy. If the pregnancies had been continued, most would no doubt have ended their education there. Instead, they had achieved a considerable improvement in their educational and occupational attainments in the years since the abortion. If they had responded to the pregnancy by marrying to provide a home for the child, they would have been making a lifelong commitment at that stage in their development to maturity. Instead, about half the women broke off their relationship with the man involved in the pregnancy, and almost half of these went on to marry someone else. Although there is no concrete evidence, one gets the impression from the women that these are more suitable, more mature marriages than would have been possible with the man involved in the pregnancy. Eight of the women married, and four plan to marry, the man who was involved. These women's lives would have been less disrupted if they had continued the pregnancy, but even they face a more favorable future because some of them have completed their education in the meantime, as have some of their husbands and fiancés, and because the decision to marry was made without the pressure of a pregnancy. Finally, seven of the women who were married at the time of the pregnancy had been divorced since that time. It is difficult to know to what extent the abortion caused the divorce or the factors that caused the divorce also caused the abortion. In any case, these women were better able to put their lives on a more satisfying basis because they did not have an infant to provide for. Abortion provides a response to unwanted pregnancy which is unpleasant and dangerous, but which apparently does not have lasting social consequences for most women.

### Second and Higher-Order Abortions

The study group was made up primarily of well-educated, intelligent, and sophisticated women; most of the women obtained medical advice on contraception after their first abortion and many changed to the most effective methods available. Yet the proportion that later found themselves again with an unwanted pregnancy, again seeking abortion, is considerable. Of the sixty-nine women who had their first abortion more than a year before the data collection, and had had enough time to test their ability to avoid unwanted pregnancy, twenty-eight, or 43 percent, had had a second abortion: of the twenty-eight who had had a second abortion and were at risk of having a third, nine, 32 percent, had done so.

Some psychiatrists and social workers believe that there is a

syndrome which they call "willful exposure to unwanted pregnancy."
One is tempted to assume that there must be a neurotic need to test
fertility after an abortion, or an unconscious wish to have children
even when the preconditions of settled married life are not possible,
or perhaps a compulsion to reenact the first traumatic experience
with abortion. Before accepting the findings of the present study
as supporting evidence for such a belief, consider some of the factors
that go into the observation of a high proportion of multiple
abortions.

First of all, there is the purely methodological point that the
study design tended to select for multiple-abortion cases. The channels of recruitment used tended to reach women who had recently
mentioned an abortion, and in most cases this was a recent one.
Women who had had only one abortion, which occurred a long
time ago, therefore, were not recruited, while women who had had
an abortion recently were accepted, whether that abortion was their
first, second, or a higher-order experience. The high proportion
of multiple abortions observed is basically an artifact of the study
design.

The fact remains that twenty-eight women have had more than
one abortion. Should these women be described as driven to do so
by psychological forces beyond their control? If we are looking
for the motivation of "willful" behavior, it is proper to consider
why these women have sexual relations and why some of them use
effective contraception. It is not equally valid to ask why women
who have sexual relations become pregnant. Consider instead how
these women could have avoided additional unwanted pregnancies.
They could have married and entered the period of life in which
pregnancies are welcome, as did many of the women who did not
have a second abortion despite considerable exposure to pregnancy.
Among those who remain at risk of unwanted pregnancy, it is contraceptive use or nonuse which is the best predictor of multiple
abortions, along with the length of time of exposure.

The question why some women have multiple abortions can be
translated into the question why some women practice effective
contraception and some do not. Part of the answer lies in the special
difficulties that unmarried women have in obtaining contraceptive
advice. Birth-control clinics usually do not accept unmarried patients,
and while there are many physicians in private practice who will
accept unmarried patients, the process of finding such a physician

presents many of the same difficulties as finding an abortionist, without the pressure of the need for an immediate solution. A number of the women in the study group told of being refused contraceptive help by physicians: one woman was refused birth-control pills by four doctors before obtaining a prescription from the fifth. A second factor is the reluctance of many unmarried women to actively seek contraceptive advice when they need it. Many of the women found it easy to avoid confrontation with the problem, relying on nonprescription methods, a vague interpretation of the rhythm method, or their sexual partner to protect them from pregnancy. Third, there are the special difficulties in using contraception experienced by women who have sexual relations only occasionally or unexpectedly. All the methods which require consistent use are difficult for these women. One of the women who obtained a prescription for the pills and yet had a second abortion explained:

> I vowed it wouldn't happen again and I carefully got the pills and took them regularly for three months. But it was ridiculous—I wasn't sleeping with anyone. I felt silly taking them so I stopped, and besides I was gaining weight. Then when I met my boyfriend and we started going together I was going to start taking them the next month, but by then I was pregnant already.

Finally, in the period when many of these pregnancies occurred there was no positively effective method available. The best methods prior to 1960 only reduced the probability of conception, to about three pregnancies per hundred woman-years of use, rather than making pregnancy impossible. Over a considerable period of time, like ten or fifteen years, the probability of at least one unwanted pregnancy occurring with the use of such contraceptives is substantial.[1] Under these circumstances, the question of why some women conceive an unwanted pregnancy and others do not may be largely a matter of chance. Many of the women claimed to have had a genuine method failure at the time of later unwanted pregnancies, and no doubt many of them did.

[1] For an analysis of the risks of unwanted conception for given levels of contraceptive effectiveness and varying lengths of time when pregnancy is unwanted, see Robert G. Potter, Jr., "Some Relationships between Short Range and Long Range Risks of Unwanted Pregnancy," *Milbank Memorial Fund Quarterly* 38 (July 1960) : 255–63.

## Summary

Observations concerning the period of the recovery from abortion and the return to normality can be summarized as follows.

1. Most of the women had no physical symptoms after the abortion other than a sense of general weakness. Most of those who reported physical symptoms said they lasted only a few days. Only two women were definitely injured by the abortion, although about one in ten women had a septic or incomplete abortion requiring treatment.

2. Somewhat less than half the women reported depression following the abortion, and 8 percent termed the depression severe.

3. About two-thirds of the women went to a physician after the abortion to obtain a check-up and routine medical care. Seventy-eight started using highly effective contraceptive methods after the abortion, and most of the others improved their methods somewhat.

4. The abortion was a time of crisis for most of the couples. Over half the women reported that their relationship with the man involved in the pregnancy got worse or deteriorated entirely. The most common complaint against the men was that they did not provide the emotional support that the women felt they needed. Few other relationships were greatly changed by the abortion.

5. Reactions to the experience can be described along a continuum from "encapsulation" of the experience to development of a politicized concern with the fate of other women who seek abortions. The majority of the women reported that they were anxious to help others, even strangers, through the difficulties of abortion if they could.

6. Women told more persons about the abortion after it was over, on the average, than they told at the time it was happening. The number told seemed to be limited by the inclusiveness of the category of those from whom the woman wished to keep her experience a secret. Women who helped many others with abortion experiences were drawn from the group that both had a high willingness to help and had few others from whom they felt they had to keep their experience a secret.

7. Most of the women recovered from physical effects within a few

days and from emotional and psychological effects within a few months. Women who gave information six months or more after the event seemed to have passed the time of great involvement in the experience, and were more concerned with other issues in their lives. In general, one gets the impression from these women that the abortion was extremely disruptive for a few months but did not have lasting social consequences for their lives, especially in comparison with the changes which would necessarily have occurred if they had continued the pregnancies.

8. Women who had second and higher-order abortions differ from the others in the length of time they have been exposed to the risk of unwanted pregnancy and in the relative ineffective contraception they practice. Unmarried women seem to have special difficulties in obtaining and using effective contraceptive techniques.

# 8

## The Flow of Information
## through the Population as a Whole

The preceding chapters have been devoted to an examination of the unique experiences of the women who contributed to this study. The warning has been given several times that it would be a serious mistake to generalize from the experience of this small group of women to the experiences of all women who have abortions by a straight projection of the present findings to all the others. We have seen that they are definitely atypical of the women of America on the basis of socioeconomic standing, education, occupation, religious affiliation, and attitudes toward abortion. In this chapter, the question of the social structure of abortion which was raised in the first chapter will be taken up again in an attempt to advance our understanding of how information about abortionists circulates in the population as a whole. In a sense, we have no more actual information on the national process available after looking at the experiences of these 114 women than we had before studying their accounts. The analysis is based on "educated guesses" rather than established facts. The experiences of the study group are the main factor that has educated the guesses made, along with the results of other studies of the society, especially studies of message transmission. For the purposes of this analysis, the women of the study group are considered as abstract entities, giving and receiving messages about abortion to and from others, without reference to the special characteristics of the givers and receivers. The women are treated as ordinary, although not necessarily typical, units in the population. The most important respect in which they differ from others, for the purposes of this analysis, is that we know a great deal about the messages they have given and received on this one isolated and relatively rare topic of message transmission, abortion, whereas very little is known about the transmission of messages on this or other topics for the population as a whole.[1]

## The Social Structure of Acquaintance Networks

Since most of the communication concerning abortion goes on in the framework of previously established acquaintance networks, a brief consideration of these networks will repay our efforts. The concept of acquaintance networks is a more refined and realistic way of handling the problem of describing the people who know one another and who influence one another than is the notion of a group or a social circle, which may have reality only in the eyes of the observer. The concept of acquaintance network defines the social universe from the point of view of a single person at a time, just as kinship analysis views a number of related people from the perspective of a specific "ego." Each person can be seen as the center of a network consisting of others who are known by the central person and who know the central person in the sense that they would recognize him on sight and would greet and speak with him if they met. Not all the people included in the acquaintance network are equally attached to the central person: one might expect to find on the order of ten to fifty family members included, and a similar number of close friends and

[1]Studies of message transmission were pioneered by Lazarsfeld, Berelson, and Gaudet with their study of voting decisions in the presidential election of 1940, reported in *The People's Choice* (New York: Columbia University Press, 1948). The hypothesis of the "two-step flow of communication" which emerges from this study served as a stimulus for further studies of the flow of information on different topics, by Merton, Katz, and Lazarsfeld; Berelson, Lazarsfeld, and McPhee; and Coleman, references to which can be found in the bibliography. This research is summarized in Elihu Katz, "The Two-Step Flow of Communication: An Up-to-Date Report on an Hypothesis," *Public Opinion Quarterly* 21 (Spring 1957): 61-78.

associates, along with a large number of more distant acquaintances such as neighbors, shopkeepers, people in the next office, fellow members of voluntary associations, people with whom one went to school, and so on.

The first research question one might wish to ask about acquaintance networks is that of sheer size or volume: How many people do people know? The research on this question is extremely laborious and time-consuming. The answer seems to be that normal American adults are acquainted with a few hundred to a few thousand others, with the figure of one thousand providing a useful estimate of the order of magnitude of the average number.[2] An extremely isolated person may know only a few hundred others well enough to speak to them or call them by their first names, while a well-known and highly active person like Franklin D. Roosevelt may have known five to ten thousand others this well. Attempts to get the women of the study group to estimate their own acquaintance universes were unsuccessful. Most of the women had never thought about it before and were at a loss to know where to begin to make a description.

Even if we knew the number of acquaintances each person can claim, we would not know much about the structure of the informal social system until we started to look at the interrelations between the networks of different people to see how they fit together. We can imagine some oversimplified ways in which it *might* fit together, which would produce very different structural effects. Imagine for a moment that each person knows exactly one thousand others, rather than something like an average of one thousand others. One way in which the acquaintance networks might fit together is into tightly bounded subgroups of 1,001 members each, with no one within a subgroup knowing anyone outside that group. Or we can imagine a pattern where each person knows all but one of the people within his subgroup and one person in another subgroup, so that the subgroups are tenuously linked. These extreme hypothetical examples lead us to think

[2]Preliminary work on the magnitude of acquaintance networks was done at M.I.T. in the early 1960s. See Michael Gurevitch, "The Social Structure of Acquaintance Networks" (Ph.D. diss., Massachusetts Institute of Technology, June 1961), and a series of unpublished papers by Ithiel Pool, F. Kochen, and others, "A Non-mathematical Introduction to a Mathematical Model"; "Contact Nets"; "The Collection of Contact Net Data"; and "Notes on the Empirical Results of the Project," 1966. The data on the acquaintance volume of F. D. Roosevelt is mentioned in these papers.

of *boundary effects* in the population, where we could draw a line and find that people are more closely tied to others on the same side of the line than they are tied to others across the line. Another simple principle on which to arrange people might be called a *neighborhood effect*. Imagine that the total population is arranged on a grid of squares like a chessboard, and each person is acquainted with all the others in the thousand squares most closely adjacent to his own. His acquaintance network will almost but not quite coincide with his neighbor's acquaintances. He will have a few people in his network that his neighbor will not have, and the neighbor will have a few that the first man does not have. Under these conditions we would not find any boundaries in the society. A message could travel through the entire population through informal channels. If the message was intended for a particular person far from the source, one might feel that the informal channels were inefficient, and regret the absence of shortcutting linkages. Imagine one more hypothetical model, for contrast, in which we envision the population in a grid with each individual linked by mutual acquaintance to one thousand others, but the choice of these others is not location in the grid but simply chance. One is no more or less likely to be acquainted with a neighbor in the grid than with any other member of the population. In this case, it could possibly happen that a random process links together the people on one side of a line and does not connect any of them to people on the other side of a line; but it would be an unlikely outcome of a random process. We would almost surely find, however, if we drew a number of lines through the grid, that more ties cross some lines than others. In other words, chance selection of acquaintances would not produce uniform connections throughout the population.

These simple models shed some light, albeit dim, on the actual form of informal social structure, which has not yet been studied in sufficient detail to provide a clear view of the actual principles on which acquaintances are organized. Whatever else we can say about it, we do know that the situation is complex. There is no single characteristic on the basis of which people form their acquaintance-ships other than physical proximity and joint participation in activities. There are a large number of formal characteristics of individuals which are related to acquaintance choices in the sense that the observed association between people with the characteristic differs from that we would expect to find if chance alone were the principle on which people selected their acquaintances.

Take the example of geography as a basis for acquaintance. We can conclude without a special study of the subject that proximity is a basis for mutual acquaintance. Any inhabited square mile in the United States will demonstrate that people within it tend to know others within it more often than they know people selected at random from outside it. The effect of geography on acquaintance networks is not uniform in all areas, however. The acquaintance networks traced in a small town will probably be far more inclusive or inbred than the networks traced in a similar area of Manhattan.[3] Despite a general tendency for the people in an area to know others on all sides of them, we would expect to find some geographical boundaries across which ties are weak or absent. Such a boundary might be a physical obstacle to movement, such as a river or a highway, or it might be more a social than a physical obstruction, like that represented traditionally by the railroad tracks in the small towns of America.

There is a long list of characteristics like location that might be related to acquaintance networks—age, sex, religion, occupation, social class, education, and political affiliation. Without being able to specify in any concrete way the exact relationship of any one of these characteristics to acquaintance networks, we can nevertheless predict that the more these characteristics refer to participation in activities as opposed to being mere status markers, the more closely we can expect the characteristic to be causally related to acquaintance networks. To take the example of education, for instance, we might expect to find a neighborhood effect; that is, people are acquainted with others who have achieved an educational level similar to their own more often than a purely chance model of acquaintanceship would predict. We would expect to find a sharper boundary between the end of one level of education like grade school or high school and the beginning of the next type of school than between any other years of education, because participation in the educational institution almost automatically involves one in making new acquaintances. We would surely find that even sharper boundaries exist between those who attended

---

[3]For a nontechnical discussion of inbreeding in networks, see Elizabeth Bott, *Family and Social Network* (London: Tavistock, 1957), especially pp. 58-61. For a more technical discussion of connectedness in networks, see Frank Harary, Robert Z. Norman, and Dorwin Cartwright, *Structural Models: An Introduction to the Theory of Directed Graphs* (New York: John Wiley & Sons, 1965), pp. 69–78.

a particular school or college and others. The causal relationship between education and acquaintanceship is participation in concrete
educational institutions and their associated activities. The correlation
of education and acquaintanceship is made up of that part which is
causally determined and an additional component contributed by the
relationship between education and other characteristics also causally
related to acquaintanceship—such as place of residence, occupation,
and participation in churches and other voluntary associations.

In contrast to education, some of the formal characteristics of individuals will tend to show pervasive boundary effects in the acquaintance networks because the characteristic applies to whole families.
Religion, race, and ethnic group membership are usually inherited
characteristics, and even the most tolerant and liberal-minded members of the group will tend to know more people within the group
than a chance association would produce, because all his relatives will
share the characteristic and the people he meets through his relatives
will tend to share the characteristic. Even in this case we will not
find the effect uniform across the society: some religious and national
origin groups interact very little with members of other groups,
whether the boundary is maintained from without by the effects of
segregation and discrimination or maintained from within by the exclusive practices of the group, while other groups maintain barely
visible or nonexistent boundaries. The boundary effects will be
strengthened, of course, by provision of special institutions like schools
and colleges maintained for members of the group.

Sociologists often use the terminology of social class as a shorthand
to discuss groups of people who are similar in status characteristics.
But whether one uses a strict definition of social class as referring only
to the relationship of the individual's source of income to the means
of production, or whether one uses a wider definition which includes
style of life and behavior aspects, and whether one considers three
major classes or makes finer distinctions into nine, twelve, or even
more "classes," one should keep in mind that a social class is not in
itself a membership group. The correlation of social class with acquaintance networks will be made up of the contribution to social
class of component status characteristics that are causally related to
acquaintance choices—such as occupation, education, and residence.
The social classes of America shade gradually into each other, and
do not show sharp boundary effects except where class lines coincide
with other bases of division such as race, ethnicity, or religion. The

concept of social class is useful in thinking about the resources available through informal channels to people in various positions in the society—the suburban wife of a professional man, the urban career girl, the slum-dwelling welfare mother, the wife of a factory worker can all be expected to know others in similar situations more often than chance would lead one to expect and will have very different access to information as well as other facilities. Yet simply calling these social-class positions skips over the problem of how social class is related to the informal social structure.

In summary, thinking of the transmission of information through informal acquaintance networks, we can at least guess that people have most access to others who resemble them in their formal characteristics, especially inasmuch as those characteristics are attained or exercised in activities and institutions. Messages started by people with a given set of social characteristics will tend to travel first and most frequently to others with similar characteristics. The kinds of paths traveled by the message will no doubt depend to some extent on the nature of the message itself. Let us turn back, therefore, to our concern with abortion information.

## The Social Structure of Abortion Communication

We have seen in examining the experiences of the women of the study group that communication concerning abortion tends to occur within the framework of the acquaintance network rather than through formal channels. This communication will involve only a portion of the acquaintance network of each person: how big a portion and what kinds of people are involved are the questions which will be examined in more detail in this chapter. The point to keep in mind while examining the flow of information through parts of the networks is that the networks themselves are developed through the normal business of living, usually without reference to an unlikely event like the need to locate an abortionist, and the connections between the networks of individuals, which determine the "direction" and accessibility of the information to others, are entirely beyond the control (and usually outside the awareness) of the individuals involved.

The questions to be examined now are: Within the framework of the acquaintance networks which exist, (1) how widely do messages about abortion circulate; that is, what is the scope of the message transmission? and (2) which persons are most likely to participate in abortion communication and which are likely to be excluded; that is, what are the major channels of the message transmission? In the final chapter of this book, we will look at some of the factors that are related to the accessibility of abortion and abortionists to various kinds of women in the population.

## The Scope of Message Transmission

The scope of message transmission refers to the sheer number of persons who are informed of each abortion that occurs, and the related question of the extent to which these tend to be the same persons who hear of many abortions or separate groups. The women of the study group provide invaluable information on the number of cases of abortion they had ever heard about from others as well as on the number of persons they had told about their own experience.

### Information Received

Let us look first at the information the women of the study group have received on the experiences of other people with abortion. The number of cases they know of because they were asked to provide help in arranging an abortion is presented in table 41. The number they heard of when the woman directly involved told them of her experience, that is, a personal confidence, is presented in table 42. The number of cases they heard about through gossip channels is pre-

TABLE 41

NUMBER OF OTHERS WHO ASKED FOR HELP

| Number Who Asked (x) | Number of Women (f) | Number of Others (x · f) |
|---|---|---|
| None | 42 | 0 |
| 1 | 41 | 41 |
| 2 | 6 | 12 |
| 3 | 4 | 12 |
| 4 | 1 | 4 |
| 5 | 4 | 20 |
| 6 | 11 | 66 |
| 7 | 1 | 7 |
| 8 | 1 | 8 |
| 12 | 2 | 24 |
| 20 | 1 | 20 |
| Total | 114 | 214 |

Note: Mean = 1.8; Median = 1.

TABLE 42

NUMBER OF OTHERS WHO PERSONALLY TOLD WOMEN
OF THEIR EXPERIENCE

| Number of Others (x) | Number of Women (f) | Number of Others (x · f) |
|---|---|---|
| None | 20 | 0 |
| 1 | 15 | 15 |
| 2 | 13 | 26 |
| 3 | 20 | 60 |
| 4 | 11 | 44 |
| 5 | 7 | 35 |
| 6 | 6 | 36 |
| 7 | 2 | 14 |
| 8 | 7 | 56 |
| 9 | 1 | 9 |
| 10 | 2 | 20 |
| 12 | 2 | 24 |
| 13 | 1 | 13 |
| 18 | 6 | 108 |
| 20 | 1 | 20 |
| Total | 114 | 480 |

sented in table 43. In each table, the number of cases represented by the messages has been projected. Thus if two women each said they knew of five cases and three women said they knew of ten, the tables show that they have mentioned forty cases of abortion among their acquaintances. There are several observations from these tables which might be noted. First, only six of the women, less than 5 percent of the group, did not know of any other people who had been involved in an abortion. Second, the number of cases known of from all sources is substantial: the average number known of by those who know of any is eleven. The 114 women recalled being told or hearing of 1,189 abortion experiences, and this number is more likely to be an underestimation due to temporary forgetting of a few cases than an overestimation. Third, the largest source of cases heard of is not requests for help or personal confidences, but second-hand accounts, or gossip.

Gossip plays an important and rather misunderstood part in informal social structure of any kind. Gossip about a person who has had an abortion, for instance, may be malicious but certainly need not be. The motivation for passing on the information might be curiosity about those involved or sympathy for their plight, shock or approval of their behavior. In any case, whatever the motives of the

TABLE 43

NUMBER OF CASES KNOWN OF BY SECONDHAND REPORT

| Number Heard of (x) | Number of Women (f) | Number of Others (x · f) |
|---|---|---|
| None | 21 | 0 |
| 1 | 8 | 8 |
| 2 | 12 | 24 |
| 3 | 14 | 42 |
| 4 | 9 | 36 |
| 5 | 8 | 40 |
| 6 | 6 | 36 |
| 7 | 2 | 14 |
| 8 | 8 | 64 |
| 9 | 1 | 9 |
| 10 | 9 | 90 |
| 11 | 1 | 11 |
| 12 | 1 | 12 |
| 16 | 1 | 16 |
| 18 | 4 | 72 |
| 20 | 5 | 100 |
| 25 | 1 | 25 |
| 30 | 2 | 60 |
| 50 | 1 | 50 |
| Total | 114 | 709 |

people who pass on gossip, it plays a significant part in disseminating information about abortion throughout the society.

Sociologists have long understood the functions of gossip in maintaining conformity to social norms: one avoids various kinds of behavior out of fear of the disapproval of others, not only those who would obviously know of the behavior but also those who would hear of it by gossip. The function of gossip in encouraging and enabling participation in illegal or deviant activities, however, has been neglected. Gossip simultaneously notifies those who disapprove of the activity in question, who can therefore avoid the person mentioned and "punish" him with disapproval, and notifies those who are interested in the activity whom they should contact in order to participate in it. The rumor that a certain person is sexually promiscuous or has access to illegal drugs, for instance, may lead some of those who hear it to shun the person and others to cultivate his acquaintance. The rumor that a certain person has had an abortion may not make that person seem attractive to those who hear it, but it may make abortion a more acceptable and comprehensible process to those who

TABLE 44

TOTAL NUMBER OF CASES OF ABORTION KNOWN OF
(SUMMARY OF TABLES 42 AND 43)

| Number of Cases (x) | Number of Women (f) | Number of Cases (x · f) |
|---|---|---|
| None | 6 | 0 |
| 1 | 4 | 4 |
| 2 | 11 | 22 |
| 3 | 12 | 36 |
| 4 | 9 | 36 |
| 5 | 4 | 20 |
| 6 | 8 | 48 |
| 7 | 8 | 56 |
| 8 | 12 | 96 |
| 9 | 4 | 36 |
| 10 | 2 | 20 |
| 12 | 5 | 60 |
| 13 | 3 | 39 |
| 14 | 1 | 14 |
| 15 | 4 | 60 |
| 16 | 1 | 16 |
| 18 | 5 | 90 |
| 22 | 1 | 22 |
| 23 | 1 | 23 |
| 25 | 1 | 25 |
| 26 | 1 | 26 |
| 27 | 1 | 27 |
| 28 | 1 | 28 |
| 32 | 1 | 32 |
| 33 | 1 | 33 |
| 34 | 1 | 34 |
| 39 | 4 | 156 |
| 60 | 1 | 60 |
| 70 | 1 | 70 |
| Total | 114 | 1,189 |

Note: Median $= 6.5$; Mean $= 10.4$; Mean number known of by those
who know of any $= 11$

have had no experience with it, may be reassuring to those who are
considering it, and may provide a source of information should the
need for abortion ever arise. This may be true even if the person who
hears it does not know the other person well, and the two never
actually discuss it. The existence of gossip serves to normalize abortion, in the sense of making it seem a normal or common occurrence,
even if it does not make abortion normative, that is, approved.

The women differ both in the number of cases of abortion they know about and the relation between the number they know of because they were personally told by those involved and those they know of by gossip. The relation between the number they were personally told of and the total number they know of may be called the "gossip factor." Its index is calculated by dividing the number of individuals who personally confided in the woman into the total number of abortion cases she knows of among her acquaintances. A gossip factor of one can be interpreted as no gossip: all the abortions the woman knows of were told to her by the person directly involved, whether that number is one or twenty. A gossip factor of two means that the woman has heard of as many abortions among her acquaintances by gossip as by personal confidences. Such an index was calculated for each of the women in the study group on the basis of her own report: the value of the index ranged from one to nine for ninety-four of the women. Twenty had an index number of infinity because they had not been personally told of any abortions. Six of these twenty had not heard of any through gossip either. These twenty women do not have a useable "gossip index" and are omitted from the analysis that requires it.

### Information Transmitted

The number of others that the women informed about their own abortion experience at various stages of the process has been presented in summary form in the relevant sections above. The complete tables of the number of others told, along with the projections of the numbers of others represented by these tellings, are presented in tables 45, 46, and 47. The phases of the process are not relevant for this analysis, but are presented in that form to show that the large numbers arrived at in table 48 were not lifted out of a hat.[4] Each woman has a number which represents the best estimate of the num-

[4]These tables differ in minor details from the summary tables which report the same information. If a woman said, for example, she had talked with ten others at one stage of her experience but described only six of them, the smaller number was used in the analysis of the kinds of people she consulted, but the larger number is used in this section. Duplications of the same persons mentioned in more than one section have been eliminated, to provide the best estimate of the total number told of the abortion. No doubt some sources of error remain. Women who were interviewed often failed to mention a few persons the first time the question was presented, and recalled them during the course of the interview: women who gave information by questionnaire may have underestimated the number they told.

TABLE 45
NUMBER OF OTHERS TOLD DURING DECISION-MAKING PHASE

| Number Told (x) | Number of Women Who Told (x) (f) | Number of Others (x · f) |
|---|---|---|
| None | 2 | 0 |
| 1 | 17 | 17 |
| 2 | 18 | 36 |
| 3 | 24 | 72 |
| 4 | 15 | 60 |
| 5 | 18 | 90 |
| 6 | 3 | 18 |
| 7 | 3 | 21 |
| 8 | 4 | 32 |
| 9 | 1 | 9 |
| 10 | 4 | 40 |
| 11 | 2 | 22 |
| 12 | 1 | 12 |
| 18 | 1 | 18 |
| 20 | 1 | 20 |
| Total | 114 | 467 |

TABLE 46
NUMBER OF OTHERS TOLD DURING SEARCH PHASE

| Number Told (x) | Number of Women Who Told (x) (f) | Number of Others (x · f) |
|---|---|---|
| None | 0 | 0 |
| 1 | 4 | 4 |
| 2 | 13 | 26 |
| 3 | 10 | 30 |
| 4 | 11 | 44 |
| 5 | 11 | 55 |
| 6 | 18* | 108 |
| 7 | 10 | 70 |
| 8 | 15 | 120 |
| 9 | 2 | 18 |
| 10 | 3 | 30 |
| 11 | 4 | 44 |
| 12 | 2 | 24 |
| 13 | 1 | 13 |
| 14 | 2 | 28 |
| 18 | 4 | 72 |
| 20 | 2 | 40 |
| 21 | 1 | 21 |
| 31 | 1 | 31 |
| Total | 114 | 778 |

*Eleven cases where the exact number was not ascertained because the woman did not know it have been placed at six, the median of the distribution.

TABLE 47

NUMBER OF OTHERS TOLD AFTER ABORTION

| Number Told (x) | Number of Women Who Told (x) (f) | Number of Others (x · f) |
|---|---|---|
| None | 11 | 0 |
| 1 | 15 | 15 |
| 2 | 10 | 20 |
| 3 | 6 | 18 |
| 4 | 12 | 48 |
| 5 | 7 | 35 |
| 6 | 5 | 30 |
| 7 | 4 | 28 |
| 8 | 1 | 8 |
| 9 | 2 | 18 |
| 10 | 2 | 20 |
| 11 | 3 | 33 |
| 12 | 3 | 36 |
| 13 | 1 | 13 |
| 15 | 4 | 60 |
| 16 | 1 | 16 |
| 18 | 2 | 36 |
| 20 | 9 | 180 |
| 22 | 1 | 22 |
| 25 | 2 | 50 |
| 30 | 2 | 60 |
| 32 | 1 | 32 |
| 34 | 1 | 34 |
| 37 | 1 | 37 |
| 39 | 2 | 78 |
| 50 | 3 | 150 |
| 55 | 1 | 55 |
| About 100 | 2 | 200 |
| Total | 114 | 1,332 |

ber of others she told of her experience up to the time of the interview, after eliminating all duplication from the lists given at various phases of the abortion process.

Table 48 shows that a large number of others were told of the experience by the women concerned: 2,577 to be as exact as possible. To expand this number to the total number of others who are likely to have heard it in any way, we must look at the effects of gossip as well as at the number told. It is probably a fair assumption that approximately the same multiplying ratio can be used to predict the number of those who have heard of our informants' experiences with abortion

TABLE 48

TOTAL NUMBER OF OTHERS TOLD OF ABORTION BY INFORMANT
(SUMMARY OF TABLES 45, 46, AND 47)

| (x) | (f) | (x · f) | (x) | (f) | (x · f) |
|-----|-----|---------|-----|-----|---------|
| 2 | 1 | 2 | 29 | 2 | 58 |
| 4 | 2 | 8 | 30 | 1 | 30 |
| 5 | 4 | 20 | 31 | 3 | 93 |
| 6 | 3 | 18 | 32 | 1 | 32 |
| 7 | 3 | 21 | 34 | 1 | 34 |
| 8 | 5 | 40 | 36 | 3 | 108 |
| 9 | 4 | 36 | 38 | 1 | 38 |
| 10 | 8 | 80 | 41 | 2 | 82 |
| 11 | 3 | 33 | 43 | 1 | 43 |
| 12 | 8 | 96 | 44 | 2 | 88 |
| 13 | 6 | 78 | 46 | 1 | 46 |
| 14 | 7 | 98 | 49 | 1 | 49 |
| 15 | 1 | 15 | 51 | 1 | 51 |
| 16 | 6 | 96 | 54 | 1 | 54 |
| 17 | 1 | 17 | 58 | 1 | 58 |
| 18 | 4 | 72 | 65 | 1 | 65 |
| 19 | 3 | 57 | 66 | 1 | 66 |
| 20 | 3 | 60 | 101 | 1 | 101 |
| 23 | 2 | 46 | 103 | 1 | 103 |
| 25 | 3 | 75 | 135 | 1 | 135 |
| 26 | 1 | 26 | | | |
| 27 | 3 | 81 | Total | 114 | 2,577 |
| 28 | 6 | 168 | | | |

Note: Median=14; Mean=22.6.

by gossip as we found existing between the number who told her personally and those she heard of. The gossip factor is probably a property of networks of people more than of individual women. Gossip is more acceptable in some circles than others, depending upon the extent to which friends of each of two persons are known to the other, and the interest with which a topic of gossip, like abortion, is viewed. For the ninety-four women for whom we could calculate a gossip factor, therefore, this index is applied as a multiplier to the number of individuals she personally told of her experience. The results are presented in table 49.

The implications of table 49 are rather startling. While the majority of the women actually told fewer than twenty persons about their experience while it was happening and afterward, the estimated average number who ever heard about the abortion is almost seventy, and may be, for an individual woman, as high as five or six hundred. We are forced to the conclusion that approximately eight thousand per-

TABLE 49

PROJECTED NUMBER OF OTHERS WHO HEARD OF ABORTIONS
BY CONFIDENCES AND GOSSIP

| Number of Others (x) | Number of Women (f) | (x · f) | Number of Others (x) | Number of Women (f) | (x · f) |
|---|---|---|---|---|---|
| 8 | 5 | 40 | 56 | 3 | 168 |
| 9 | 1 | 9 | 66 | 1 | 66 |
| 10 | 2 | 20 | 69 | 1 | 69 |
| 12 | 3 | 36 | 72 | 1 | 72 |
| 13 | 2 | 26 | 74 | 1 | 74 |
| 14 | 1 | 14 | 78 | 1 | 78 |
| 16 | 2 | 32 | 81 | 1 | 81 |
| 17 | 1 | 17 | 82 | 1 | 82 |
| 19 | 1 | 19 | 84 | 1 | 84 |
| 20 | 3 | 60 | 96 | 1 | 96 |
| 22 | 1 | 22 | 99 | 1 | 99 |
| 24 | 2 | 48 | 101 | 1 | 101 |
| 25 | 2 | 50 | 103 | 1 | 103 |
| 26 | 2 | 52 | 104 | 1 | 104 |
| 27 | 1 | 27 | 112 | 1 | 112 |
| 28 | 1 | 28 | 114 | 2 | 228 |
| 30 | 2 | 60 | 117 | 1 | 117 |
| 32 | 2 | 64 | 138 | 2 | 276 |
| 33 | 2 | 66 | 140 | 1 | 140 |
| 36 | 3 | 108 | 143 | 1 | 143 |
| 37 | 1 | 37 | 144 | 1 | 144 |
| 38 | 1 | 38 | 170 | 1 | 170 |
| 39 | 1 | 39 | 180 | 1 | 180 |
| 41 | 1 | 41 | 186 | 1 | 186 |
| 42 | 5 | 210 | 246 | 1 | 246 |
| 44 | 1 | 44 | 292 | 1 | 292 |
| 45 | 1 | 45 | 375 | 1 | 375 |
| 48 | 2 | 96 | 606 | 1 | 606 |
| 52 | 1 | 52 | Total | 87* | 6,014 |
| 54 | 1 | 54 | | | |

Note: Mean = 69.13; Median = 42

*Twenty women were omitted from this table because a meaningful "gossip ratio" could not be calculated, and seven more were omitted due to inadequacies in the data on the number of others told of the experience.

sons have heard about the abortions experienced by these 114 women. From this perspective, the fact that they have received over two hundred requests for help from others seeking abortion in the average of four years that have elapsed since their first abortion experience does not seem particularly high. These eight thousand persons are not, however, necessarily all different individuals: as we saw in table 44, a single person may receive information on as many as seventy different abortions. Rather than try to calculate how many of the women in the study group confided in the same persons, let us use the results of this analysis for a speculative analysis of how many messages concerning abortion are transmitted and held by the entire population of the United States.

The calculation is simple enough. There is some number, $x$, of cases of abortion which have occurred to women in the reproductive years. Each of these cases was reported to some number of other persons, $y$, by confidences and gossip. The mean number of others informed of each case is $\bar{y}$. The number of messages generated by all of these abortions is $x \cdot \bar{y}$. Let us guess that there have been ten million intentional abortions over the years to women who are now in the reproductive years. Each of these abortions generated some number of messages. To be on the conservative side, let us assume that the average number who ever hear of an individual abortion is overestimated by the women in the study group: they can be assumed to be less secretive about their experience than the average person, since they volunteered to be in a study. On the average, let us say, fifty persons rather than seventy will have heard of each abortion that has occurred. The total number of messages generated will be five hundred million. Clearly this does not refer to five hundred million different persons, as there are not that many available to hear about them. Looking back to table 44 we see that the average number of cases known of by a woman who knows of any is eleven. We therefore divide the number of messages by eleven to estimate how many different individuals they went to. This calculation suggests that in the nation as a whole, somewhat more than forty-five million persons know of one or more abortion. There are about two hundred million Americans. We can safely discount those under fifteen and over fifty, as abortion is a concern of people in the reproductive years. The population between fifteen and fifty includes roughly one hundred million persons, so our estimate implies that about 45 percent of the adults know of one or more cases of abortion among their acquaintances.

Let us say that the messages about these abortions go equally to men and women, which is consistent with the experiences of the women of the study group. The fifty million adult women of America, then, would have received 250,000,000 messages, and we estimate that 22,500,000 know of at least one abortion. Since only six of the 114 who contributed to the study group did not know of anyone else who had had an abortion, we can estimate a 95 percent overlap between the ten million women who have had an abortion and the women who hear about one or more of those which occur. The estimated number of women, then, who know of at least one abortion, including their own, if any, is approximately twenty-three million out of fifty million. More than half the women, therefore, will not know of any abortions among their acquaintances if the assumptions made are correct.[5]

To say that somewhat less than half the women know of one or more cases of abortion among their acquaintances is not to say that all such people could arrange an abortion if they chose to do so. Many of those who know of a case of abortion will not know anything except the plain fact that a certain woman has had an abortion. Many of these cases will have occurred some time ago, and the source of the abortion may no longer be available, as abortionists seem to change their location or retire from practice with considerable frequency. The rate at which information "decays" by the abortionist's changing his address or ending his practice is not known. The impression obtained from this study is that a lead obtained more than two or three years previously is no longer useful in most instances. In any case, the participants in the distribution of information have no control over the length of time that an address remains useful. In addition, some sources of abortion are not available to anyone who learns of the address and has the necessary amount of money. Some practitioners select their clients from those who come to them, and only perform abortions for certain people. Other sources are so incompetent or dangerous that the women who used them originally would not give the address to others, so that knowing of their experience will not help anyone to obtain access to an abortionist. Perhaps less than

[5]These figures, of course, are based on bald-faced assumptions and parameters computed from incomplete data. The relationship proposed is simply

$$\frac{x \cdot \bar{y}}{\bar{z}} = \text{the number in the reproductive age group who know of one or more abortions}$$

where $x =$ the number of abortions that have already occurred; $y =$ the number informed of each abortion that has occurred, and $\bar{y} =$ the mean of that distribution; $z =$ the number of cases of abortion known of by those who know of any, and $\bar{z} =$ the mean of that distribution. The example sets $x$ at ten million, which implies an abortion rate of two-thirds of a million *first* abortions per year, and an accumulated incidence of abortion of roughly 20 percent of the women in the reproductive years. The mean of $y$ is set at fifty and the mean of $z$ is set at eleven. Readers who enjoy it may wish to work out the implications of their own guesses of these parameters.

half of those who know of a person who has had an abortion could use that information to gain contact with an abortionist if the need arose.

The picture that emerges, therefore, is that all the information concerning access to abortionists is concentrated in a minority of the population, and that a substantial proportion of even that minority has access only to an obsolete source or one active source at best. Without the process of an active search for an abortionist, most people have little or no choice to offer to themselves or to someone who comes to them for help in arranging an abortion. When an active search is conducted by a person who is not embarrassed to ask for help and is not willing simply to take the first lead that appears, the information available can be concentrated and collated, making possible something like a rational choice between the alternative abortionists who are available. When this is done, and it seems to be done as often by self-appointed "abortion specialists" who are not in the process of obtaining an abortion as by a woman or a couple who are motivated to find the best source of an abortion for themselves, those who locate this source of information have considerable choice. In general, however, very little choice is exercised in the selection of abortionists.

## The Channels of Message Transmission: Barriers to the Flow of Information

Some portions of acquaintance networks are closed to the flow of information about abortion, because one person strongly objects to the practice, because the relationship between the individuals is such that they cannot discuss the topic, or because the channel is so rarely used and superficial that such a message would be inappropriate. The women of the study group contributed information to the question who these various people are by their answers to the questions: (1) "Are there any particular people that you would *not* want to talk with about abortion?" and (2) "Are there any people that you are particularly anxious should *not* find out about your experience?"

Table 50 summarizes the data on barriers to the flow of information between the informants and the people around them. In general it appears that the barriers to free flow of information are located (1) within the kinship area of the acquaintance universe, particularly across generational lines; (2) across authority lines, exemplified where women mentioned employers, teachers, school authorities,

TABLE 50

BARRIERS TO THE FLOW OF INFORMATION

Number of Women Who Mentioned at Least One Person in
Category as a Person with Whom She Would Not Want to Talk
of Abortion (in General), or from Whom She Was Keeping
Her Own Abortion a Secret

| Relationship | Would Not Want to Talk | | Keeping Own Experience Secret | |
|---|---|---|---|---|
| | N | Rank | N | Rank |
| Mother or parents | 57 | (1) | 49 | (1) |
| Brother, sister, or cousin | 12 | (4) | 3 | (9) |
| Neighbor(s) | 18 | (3) | 6 | (8) |
| Own children | 5 | (9) | 13 | (3) |
| A close friend | 7 | (7) | 8 | (5) |
| Husband, boyfriend | 4 | (10) | 12 | (4) |
| Male friends | 6 | (8) | 7 | (6½) |
| Own doctor, family doctor | 0 | (11) | 0 | (11) |
| Co-workers | 11 | (5) | 27 | (2) |
| People who disapprove, Catholics | 35 | (2) | 7 | (6½) |
| Police, law-enforcement agencies | 10 | (6) | 2 | (10) |

Note: N = 114.

and subordinates such as pupils and employees; and (3) at some
social distance, barring communication with people with whom the
women does not have an intimate relationship, such as neighbors or
"someone you work with." Peer-aged relatives are less likely to be
included in the open flow of information than friends, but are more
likely to be sources of information or confidants than either the
woman's parents or her own children.

Cross-cutting the weak barriers to the flow of information which
appear at some social distance from the woman and the more substantial barriers which isolate kin from hearing about the abortion
are barriers which follow generational or age-grade lines. These barriers tend to be very strong in the area of the nuclear family and
weaker at some distance, but are in evidence in most reports. One's
own parents and one's own children are the sources of most concern
about keeping the abortion secret, but many of the women mentioned
"older people" or "younger people" in general as well. Some gave as
their reason that these older or younger people would be more likely
to tell members of their own families, but others indicated that they

do not talk about intimate matters with people outside their own age group. Eighteen women volunteered that they do not talk to their family friends or older people in general about abortion, because they are old-fashioned or would not understand. Others mentioned religious people in answer to the same question, and some of these indicated by their reasons that they had older people in mind.

Age-grading of the flow of information implies that the practices concerning abortion can change radically very quickly. The decline of knowledge of effective "folk methods" for use by the pregnant woman or a nonspecialist, for instance, may be a product of this age-grading of information, as older women stopped passing on their techniques to younger women.[6] Older women can continue using more difficult or dangerous methods of abortion, while women a generation younger may have access to better resources. It is probably more common that the older women have developed good resources for locating competent doctors over the years, while their daughters and the neighbors' daughters may only be able to locate resources which the older women have long since discarded.

While relatively few of the women obtained help from their mothers or another older woman, the cases in which this happens may have structural importance for the distribution of information in excess of

[6]The vague knowledge of "folk methods" of abortion reported by the women in the study group stands in contrast to the results of a recent study in England which suggests that nonmedical methods are well known and frequently used by working-class women, who go to another woman, usually considerably older, in the same neighborhood for nonmedical abortions. See Moya Wood-wide, "Attitudes of Women Abortionists," *Family Planning*, vol. 12, no. 2 (July, 1963). It is difficult to know whether this is a national difference in abortion practices or primarily a result of the high socioeconomic standing of the majority of women in the study group. In the United States, folk methods have been reported by Newman to be more frequently known by "clinic patients" than the private patients of physicians in her sample. See Lucile Newman, "Abortion as Folk Medicine," *California Health*, October–November, 1965, pp. 75–79. The Kinsey group report found folk knowledge more prevalent among Negroes than whites, although they felt that most of these methods were ineffective. See Paul Gebhard *et al.*, *Pregnancy, Birth and Abortion* (New York: Harper & Bros. and Paul H. Hoeber, Inc., 1958). For reports of techniques of abortion used by people around the world who do not have access to medical facilities, see Herbert Aptekar, *Infanticide, Contraception and Abortion in Savage Society* (New York: Wm. Godwin, 1931); George Devereaux, *A Study of Abortion in Primitive Societies* (New York: Julian Press, 1955); and Norman E. Himes, *Medical History of Contraception* (Baltimore: Williams & Wilkins, 1936).

the numbers represented, as the information is not only used to help an individual member of the younger generation but may come into circulation among the younger women and thereafter be available to them without the necessity of consulting someone in the older generation.

Positively, then, what are the channels through the acquaintance networks in which communication about abortion is likely to circulate? Both numerically and socially, the most important channels are intimate "friends"—equal-age and equal-status contacts between people who voluntarily associate with each other, sharing leisure-time activities. The similar phrasing but different meanings of the terms "girl friend" and "boyfriend" are suggestive in this context. Many of the women gave the impression that they could talk freely with a number of other women about abortion, which of course implies an acknowledgment of sexual relations, but could only speak freely with men with whom they actually had a sexual relationship. Among most of the unmarried women, then, the information seems to be conveyed to girl friends, who in turn tell their boyfriends, and to current and sometimes later boyfriends of the woman directly involved. Among married women, of course, the husband plays the same role of confidant as the boyfriend does for the unmarried woman. No men were interviewed in the course of this study, so we have no information on the question whether men have a mirror image of this pattern, of talking freely with a number of intimate same-sex friends but only with members of the opposite sex with whom they actually have a sexual relationship.

In any case, the analysis suggests that information is likely to circulate primarily among the equal-age, equal-status acquaintances that people call friends, while those who have either an authority relationship or a distant, nonintimate relationship are excluded from communication. This does not, of course, mean that the individuals who stand in such a relationship to one are excluded from all informal communication concerning abortion. Relationships are relative to a given ego, and we guess that the same person is a part of the acquaintance network of about a thousand people, in various roles. The individual in question may well have intimate friends of his own, who will inform him of any information that happens to be available from that direction. It does mean that abortion events in certain parts of one's acquaintance network are likely to be invisible to one. The number of abortions one does happen to know of reflects something about the incidence of abortion among one's intimate friends and perhaps the friends of one's friends and not about the incidence in the acquaintance network as a whole.

## Communication through Formal Channels

Communication leaves the informal structure of acquaintance networks and enters the formal structure when people are told of the abortion on the basis of their professional or occupational standing, whether or not the teller happens to have been previously acquainted with the person told. The major recipients of abortion information through formal channels are doctors, as we have seen. Women approach doctors, either their own doctors, one recommended by a friend, or a total stranger, to ask for confirmation of the unwanted pregnancy, to ask for an abortion or advice in getting an abortion, and to have a physical examination after an abortion has been performed. These communications, which are only a minority of the communications about abortion, have two special functions worth noting.

First, random requests to physicians for help in terminating an unwanted pregnancy may play an important role in the recruitment of physicians into abortion practice. Each abortionist must have a first case or a first few cases before the informal communication network can pick up his address and provide it to people seeking abortion. A doctor who is not adverse to performing abortions and who would be glad to have the large amounts of money involved need not go out looking for business. All doctors, especially those in private practice, can expect to receive a request to perform an abortion sooner or later. A physician whose name comes first alphabetically in the listing of specialists in obstetrics and gynecology in a major city reports that he receives tentative requests from strangers with great regularity. Most physicians refuse these requests for help and there are no further consequences to the communication. People don't seem to pass on the information that a certain doctor is not sympathetic. If he should later change his mind for some reason and decide to accept abortion patients, he can realistically expect to be approached by others in the course of time.

The second important function of communication with physicians is that it keeps the physicians informed and aware to some extent of the scope of the problem of illegal abortion in America. If the informal communication system worked perfectly to supply abortions to those who want them, the process would be completely invisible in formal channels except in the rare case of the death of a patient or the arrest of a practitioner. The fact that most women inform at least one reputable physician of their experience with abortion keeps the doctors aware that respectable, likeable women, of the kind the doctor is dedicated to serving with his medical skill, find the problem of un-wanted pregnancy insupportable without the adjunct of abortion as a last resort. If the reform of the abortion laws and procedures occurs, as now seems to be happening in many localities, physicians will necessarily play a major part in demanding reforms and in carrying out the new plans that are approved. The frequently awkward re-quests that women make to doctors for help with abortion, which often seem so painful and futile from the woman's point of view, nevertheless play a necessary part in insuring that doctors are able and willing to play their necessary role in easing the inequities and dangers of the present system.

# 9

## *Differential Access to Abortion and Abortionists*

This chapter will be concerned with the answers to three questions. First, what are the circumstances in which some women decide that a pregnancy is intolerable? or, when is a pregnancy defined as unwanted? Second, among those women who find themselves with an unwanted pregnancy, what are the factors that determine the outcome of the pregnancy—why do some women seek abortion and others not? Finally, among those women who do seek abortion, what are the factors that determine which women obtain legal abortions and which obtain various types of illegal abortions? The present study does not provide empirical answers to these questions, but does suggest some of the factors that may be involved and that may be worth further consideration and study.

### When Is a Pregnancy Defined as Unwanted?

Raising the question of when a given pregnancy is defined as unwanted, a doctor, speaking at a Planned Parenthood-sponsored conference on abortion, said:

Much has been said about the unwanted child and I would like to know exactly when a parent or a doctor decides that a child is unwanted. I think Dr. Kinsey would agree that there would be a considerable discrepancy about the answer the parents would give concerning whether a child was wanted or not, whether the poll was taken one month before conception, the night of conception, a night two months after conception when the mother is vomiting and the other children have the croup, or the day after delivery when the mother has the child in her arms. I am not sure when the child is unwanted and I'm not sure that anyone else is either.[1]

Another doctor answered him by assuring him that the individuals involved are often absolutely certain when a given pregnancy is unwanted.

A large part of my practice is concerned with helping the infertile couple, and I know the terrific frustration of a woman who wants a child and cannot have one. It does not compare with the intensity of emotion and determination of the woman who does not want a child, is pregnant, and *won't have it*. I have learned that such a woman, on the private practice level, determined to have an abortion, usually finds some way of getting it.[2]

Both of these doctors point out important truths about unwanted pregnancy. In order to be entirely happy about a pregnancy, a woman should ideally have a happy marriage, robust health, and a generous supply of the things that a child will require—financial security, time and energy, and affection. If any of these elements are absent, the woman might well consider the pregnancy unwanted; yet we know that many do not or only do so temporarily.

In general we can say that the decision whether a pregnancy is wanted or unwanted depends upon an interaction between the circumstances of the pregnancy and the values and beliefs of the individuals involved. Some women, probably a very small proportion of the population, would reject any pregnancy that occurred under any circumstances, while others would require extremely difficult circumstances before rejecting a pregnancy and others would not reject a pregnancy under any circumstances at all. The present study suggests that it is more fruitful to think about the amount of differ-

---

[1]Joseph P. Donnelly, speaking at the Arden House Conference on Abortion, 1955, in Mary Calderone, ed. *Abortion in the United States* (New York: Harper and Bros. and Paul H. Hoeber, Inc., 1958).

[2]Sophia Kleegman, *ibid.*

ence the birth of a child would make in the life of the mother and the extent to which a new child would hurt the interests of the people she cares about rather than about particular elements like marriage or financial security that are missing from the formula for a happy pregnancy. While individual women will vary in their personal reactions to an unexpected pregnancy, the kinds of situations that occur can be tentatively ranked on the basis of the predicted proportion of women in the groups who would consider a pregnancy unwanted. The following list is proposed as a rank order of the most probably rejected pregnancies to the least probably rejected ones.

1. Previously married women with children, especially if living on alimony or other support from their previous husband.
2. Unmarried career women, whether single or previously married, who support themselves.
3. Unmarried women who conceive by a man they cannot marry or do not want to marry.
4. Women who believe that their marriage is ended, who are contemplating divorce.
5. Married women who have reached their desired family size, especially if their youngest child is already in school and the mother has adjusted her style of life by work or other activities so that it is no longer compatible with the intensive care of a preschool child.
6. Women who are newly married or about to be married who have plans which preclude children, such as finishing their education, which they want to carry out before having a child.
7. Women who have started their family and have not yet reached their desired family size.

Two other situations which are often mentioned in discussions of abortion and the problem of unwanted pregnancy are not included in the list because they are entirely different from the kinds of situations discussed here. A pregnancy conceived by forcible rape would probably head the list as the most often unwanted, but it is such an unlikely event that it is not really relevant to an understanding of the reasons why women define certain pregnancies as unwanted. The second case, in which a pregnancy would probably result in a seriously deformed child if it were continued, as when the mother has had rubella (German measles) during the first three months of pregnancy, is excluded because it is not the pregnancy which is unwanted but the deformity of the child. A mother might decide to terminate such a pregnancy, often on the advice of a physician, without being in a situation where pregnancy as such was unwanted.

The contribution that each of these groups makes to the pool of unwanted pregnancies depends not only on the probability that a given pregnancy will be considered unwanted, but on the size of these groups and the success with which the women in them use contraceptive methods to prevent pregnancy. The fifth group mentioned, for instance, composed of married women who have had all the children they wish to have, is fairly low on the list of the probability that a pregnancy will be considered unwanted, but probably makes a large contribution to the number of unwanted pregnancies because there are so many women in the group.

### The Choice of Abortion as Opposed to Alternative Responses to Unwanted Pregnancy

The alternatives to abortion, given that an unwanted pregnancy has occurred, might be a hasty marriage, illegitimacy, giving up the child for adoption, or simply incorporating the child into an already existing family.[3] The women of the study group, however, made it clear that they did not perceive the whole range of alternatives in any single case. In general, the single women who conceived with a serious boyfriend thought only of abortion or marrying the man, while single women who conceived in a casual affair thought only of abortion, illegitimacy, or adoption. None of the married or previously married women entertained the idea of adoption. Whether or not it is legally possible for such a woman to give a child up for adoption, they did not perceive that option as open to them.

In general, the present study suggests that the major factor which

---

[3]Both illegitimacy and premaritally conceived, maritally terminated pregnancies are more common than many people realize. A recent study conducted among a random sample of Detroit families showed that between a quarter and a third of the first marriages of white couples involved a premarital pregnancy, and an even higher proportion of marriages of nonwhites. See William F. Pratt, "Pre-marital Pregnancies and Illegitimate Births in a Metropolitan Community—An Analysis of Age and Color Differentials," paper delivered at the meetings of the Population Association of America, April 1965; and T. P. Monahan, "Premarital Pregnancy in the United States," *Eugenics Quarterly* 7 (1960): 133-47.

determines how a woman will react to an unwanted pregnancy is her perception of what others in her visible social universe do in such a case. Most of the women in the study group knew of several others who had had abortions, and knew that abortion is one of the accepted alternatives to an unwanted pregnancy among the people important to them. Abortion may not be generally approved of or highly valued among those the woman knows, but it is seen as a necessary evil in some situations.

Similarly other women, who do not appear in the study group, find alternatives to abortion highly visible around themselves. An estimated one-quarter to one-third of contemporary urban marriages involve a premarital pregnancy.[4] A woman whose girl friends, sisters, and cousins have married during pregnancy will have little embarrassment or hesitation about doing the same, providing that the man involved is willing to marry her. A Catholic woman who is surrounded by other women who have large families may be inconvenienced by an additional pregnancy, but is unlikely to seriously consider the possibility of abortion if none of her friends and neighbors do. Negro women, who make up only about 12 percent of the population, have more than half of all the illegitimate births that occur each year, and an individual woman may accept the possibility of raising a fatherless child with little difficulty.

No doubt the most stressful situation is that of a woman who has never heard of an acknowledged unwanted pregnancy among the people she knows and respects. A woman who has grown up believing that only people who are prepared to have children have sexual intercourse is in an intolerable position if she finds herself pregnant and unable to marry. The homes for unwed mothers which shelter women while their pregnancy is obvious and quietly arrange for the adoption of the child after birth are designed to help this kind of woman. The woman often leaves her local community, sometimes going to a distant part of the country, while the people at home are told that she is away at school, visiting a relative, or taking a trip to Europe. When the baby is born and given up for adoption, she can return home with her secret well hidden. Other women may give up on the possibility of returning to their homes, and go to a new community to live and have their babies, sometimes

---

[4]Probably many of these couples consider a premarital pregnancy somewhat embarrassing but not unwanted.

assuming a married name and a fictitious husband. No doubt some actually kill themselves: more only consider it. Some of the women in the study group were in this situation. These women tended to be passive about arranging the abortion, in most cases leaving it entirely to the man involved in the pregnancy to make decisions and arrangements, and tending to be deeply resentful toward him over the unpleasant aspects of the abortion. Abortion is an invisible solution to unwanted pregnancy in the sense that people who are not told cannot detect the pregnancy or the aftereffects, and a woman who is desperate for an invisible solution may be grateful if an abortion can be arranged without requiring that she take much initiative. Whatever she does, if she succeeds in keeping the pregnancy a secret and her solution invisible, she will not influence others in her social circle who encounter a similar problem at a later time.

The responses to unwanted pregnancy will be clustered in informal social networks just as routes to particular abortionists are clustered through acquaintance networks. The alternatives chosen by individual women will structure the alternatives available to those who come after them in having unwanted pregnancies in the manner of votes cast for the acceptability of the various alternatives. A few women who have an openly acknowledged illegitimate pregnancy and birth will increase the probability of that solution being used by others who know them personally. Similarly, a few women who have an induced abortion and talk freely about their experience with their acquaintances will make abortion more probable for all those who hear, directly or indirectly, of the experience, when an unwanted pregnancy occurs.

## Social Class and the Outcome of Unwanted Pregnancies

I believe that social class is related to the individual's response to an unwanted pregnancy, but that the relationship is complex rather than simple. Social class categories are too large and inclusive in themselves to be of much help in predicting the response to an unwanted pregnancy. The wife of a factory worker and a high-school dropout working as a store clerk may both be considered working-class, a rural farm owner's wife and a suburban business owner's wife are both middle class, and a successful career woman and a debutante are both upper-class, without, however, having much in common. The relation between social class and the outcome of unwanted pregnancy is modified by the age and reproductive history of the woman, her marital status, the reasons the pregnancy is unwanted, and her ethnic background, religion, and degree of religious commitment.

We should also consider the possibility that the outcome of unwanted pregnancy is a factor in determining class position rather than the opposite. Possession of an illegitimate child in the home may be a major determinant of being lower class, not only because of the attitudes toward an unwed mother but because of the loss of opportunities for maintaining status that having a child entails. Caring for the child deprives the mother of the opportunity to pursue a job or improve her education, and the public welfare or Aid to Dependent Children relief which makes it possible to live and care for the child insures a lower-class standing in the community. Similarly, marrying under the pressure of pregnancy seems to be a major factor in lowering the socioeconomic standing of families. Freedman and Coombs, in a recent study of the effects of child spacing on family income, savings, and debt, found that about 20 percent of their sample of Detroit families had been premaritally pregnant.[5] Premarital pregnancy rates were as high among the couples who had a middle-class parental background as among those with a lower status background. The striking finding of their study was the high association between the economic standing of the family *after* marriage and the premarital pregnancy rate. The lower the current family income, the higher the percentage of couples who had a premarital pregnancy. Their interpretation of the finding is that the need for immediate income and security constrains the husband in his choice of jobs and his ability to pursue promotion. Whatever the cause of the association, they report, it does not disappear even after eight or nine years of marriage.

We should also keep in mind that the choice of a response to unwanted pregnancy is undoubtedly related to the opportunities available to women in various positions in the society, but we should be careful not to think of these "opportunities" exclusively in terms of money or the things money can buy. It is tempting to summarize the situation by the proposition that the rich can buy

[5] Ronald Freedman and Lolagene Coombs, "Childspacing and Family Economic Position," *American Sociological Review* 31 (October 1966) : 631-48.

their way out of trouble while the poor have to suffer the consequences—"the rich get richer and the poor get children"—but this
formulation ignores the very large part played by individual decisions as to the most moral course of action, which it has been
argued is related to observation of what others in the immediate
social environment do in such a case, and access to information
about how to go about carrying out the various alternatives such
as abortion. Neither of these factors is directly related to the possession of money, status, or power. Given that a person has decided
to seek abortion to end an unwanted pregnancy and has some information about how to go about it, these factors may play an
important role in the quality of the abortion she obtains.

## Access to Various Kinds of Abortions

What are the factors that determine which women obtain legal
abortions and which obtain various types of illegal abortions? The
resources available to the women who participated were not very
different. Most of them had friends who were willing to help, levels
of education, sophistication, and assurance that should help, and
access to the necessary amounts of money. Yet we have already
seen that the type of treatment they obtained varied from highly
skillful and considerate treatment by physicians working with assistants in modern hospitals and clinics to dangerous and degrading
experiences provided by unclean and untrained abortionists in hotels,
motels, or private homes.

The difference is not merely one of money. Better treatment tends
to be more expensive, but it is not consistently so. Some of the
women who received inadequate care paid far more than others who
obtained excellent care. Other women would have cheerfully paid
higher prices, even if it meant borrowing money, for better treatment if it had been available.

When other things are equal, competent, considerate, conveniently
located, and inexpensive abortionists will flourish and incompetent
or other generally unattractive competitors will not find any clients.
It is safe to assume that no one accepts bad treatment when she
could get better treatment, and there is no reason for thinking that
women do not receive an honest, if ill-informed, appraisal of the
qualities of abortionists they hear about. The women who receive

bad treatment have no choice, or only a choice between equally unattractive alternatives.

With these considerations in mind, let us look back at the experiences reported by the women in the study group to see if we can isolate some of the factors that lead women to the different types of abortions. From most unattractive and dangerous to most safe and convenient, these types are (1) self-induced abortions, (2) catheter-type abortions, performed by someone other than a physician, (3) D. and C. operations performed by a physician but without anesthesia, (4) D. and C. operations performed with anesthesia, and (5) legal hospital abortions. Within types, it is still true that practitioners will vary in the degree of skill, consideration, and the prices charged.

The crucial factor in determining the kind of care received is the connections or channels one is able to locate and use within the four-to-ten-week period between the recognition of pregnancy and the time when abortion becomes difficult and dangerous. The problem for the woman is to find a person who links her, however distantly, to the referral network of an abortionist. Beyond that immediate goal, she naturally wishes to find a point of linkage not just to any abortionist but to the one who is most competent, conveniently located, inexpensive, and considerate. All the women reached their first goal of finding someone: some reached good abortionists as well. There is an element of social skill in the ability to find and utilize such channels, but it is minor compared to the importance of other, more structural, aspects of the position of the woman relative to the referral networks and the acquaintance networks she has to work with, and odd factors which might best be described simply as luck.

*Norms concerning Induced Abortion*

Rossi's recent study indicates that most Americans do not think abortion should be legally available to most women.[6] In chapters 4 and 5, however, it was shown that most of the people that these women consulted did approve of abortion in this particular case, and many tried to help to arrange it. This contradiction can be partly explained by the difference between a general attitude and

[6]Alice S. Rossi, "Public Views on Abortion," Unpublished paper, Committee on Human Development, University of Chicago, February 1966.

a specific situation. No doubt many of the people who gave help do not approve of abortion in general, and may continue to disapprove after giving help in a particular case. The instance need only be defined as an exception, and the contradiction disappears. It is also undoubtedly true that these women selected the poeple who were most likely to approve of abortion or to be willing to consider them an exceptional case, in asking for help and advice.

It remains true, however, that there are large differences in the proportion of all people in a network who approve of abortion or who are willing to bend their standards to meet an individual case. Compare the situation of two women in the study group. The first is an unreligious college student, from a liberal Jewish background, living in the East Village in New York. She shares an apartment with her boyfriend who is an artist. The second woman, who lives within a few miles of the first and is almost the same age, is the mother of three children and separated from her husband. She comes from a religious Catholic family, and spends most of her free time with her children and other relatives, most of whom live in the same apartment building. Both of these women had a difficult time arranging an abortion. The first asked twenty people for help before she located an abortionist, and mentioned the pregnancy to many others, before and after the abortion was performed. She did not tell anyone who opposed her decision, and it did not occur to her that this was a possibility. She kept the abortion secret from her parents so that they would not worry about her. The second woman feared that learning of the pregnancy or the abortion would "kill" her family. She told no one among the people she is closest to. The abortion was arranged through a distant acquaintance who worked in the same office, who happened to come in and find her crying in the ladies' room at the office.

In the first case, probably 98 percent of the people in the acquaintance network had no objection to abortion. In the second case, probably more like 2 percent were similarly liberal. These are extreme cases: the point is that there are very large ranges within which the proportion who can be drawn on for help can vary.

*Openness of Communication*
One aspect of the normative position on abortion is the attitudes which people express when they are asked about it. Another aspect is the extent to which it is discussed at all. Fifty-four women re-

ported that abortion is definitely a rare topic of discussion among people they know, while twenty said it depended entirely on the circumstances and forty said it was a fairly common topic of conversation at least in certain circles to which they belong. Women for whom abortion is an easy and casual topic of conversation will have less difficulty approaching others for help if the need arises, and are likely to find more help available from those they ask.

*Kinds of Networks*

People do not, ordinarily, take any account of such a rare event as abortion in developing their circle of friends and acquaintances. Nevertheless, the history of their associations will have a great deal of influence on the resources available to them at the time of an abortion.

Three types of networks worth mentioning emerged from the accounts of the women of the study group: the woman who has maintained a consistent pattern of association with others throughout her life, a "traditional" pattern; the woman who has left her family home and community to live among mostly unmarried people; and the unusual situation in which a woman has made her interest in abortion a part of her social life, through participation in abortion-law reform groups.

A traditional network is one which is continuous over the lifetime of its central figure, is based primarily on kinship and geography, and includes people at all stages of the life cycle. The Catholic woman mentioned above can be described as living in a traditional network. She was born and grew up in the same neighborhood: her social world consists of her relatives, her co-workers, her friends from school and their families, and her neighbors. It also includes some more distant acquaintances like the woman who helped arrange her abortion.

A traditional network can be relatively open or closed to information about abortion. A woman living in such a social situation may find it easy or difficult to terminate a pregnancy. The point is not that traditional networks restrict the availability of information about abortion, but that a woman who has such a network will have little ability to control whether she receives a great deal of information or no information.

Many of the women who contributed to this study can be described as living in bachelor networks. In fact, the women have spent an average of almost six years living independently of their parents before their marriages, if any. Most of these have retained their ties with their parents and some of their best friends from the communities in which they grew up, but have moved to large cities or college communities to follow opportunities for education, for occupational advances, and for the style of life which they find congenial.

Concentrations of young unmarried people and previously married people simplify the task of transmitting information about abortion by providing contact between people with high risks of needing abortion and people who are likely to have already had such an experience. Attitudes toward extramarital pregnancy and abortion are likely to be liberal in such communities, and the fact that membership is transient and often drawn from widely dispersed sources tends to encourage a free flow of information.

Friendship networks formed around participation in the activities of abortion-reform societies are rare but are of particular interest for the flow of information. Women who participate in these activities and develop friendships from within the circle of people met during activities no doubt have the greatest concentration of information about abortion and abortionists to be found anywhere in the society. It is unusual to be able to locate people on the basis of their special interest in the subject of abortion: abortion-reform societies provide an opportunity to do just that.

### Inbreeding of Networks

"Inbreeding" or "inchoosing" is the extent to which people within a network as defined by one person are connected to each other as well as to the central person. Both the Catholic woman and the student living with her boyfriend in New York have relatively highly inbred networks: their friends tend to know each other. On the other hand a married woman cataloged her resources for finding an abortionist as follows: friends from her home town whom she was still in contact with, a few friends from each of the two colleges she had attended, friends from the job she had before her marriage, and people at her husband's place of work. While there was inbreeding within each of these groups, there was no overlap, other than herself, linking the people from these different contexts. If this woman had been unable to find an abortionist through one channel, she could have tried another "fresh start" which might lead her to entirely different information networks.

Inbreeding explains the persistence of use of poorly qualified or expensive abortionists while more attractive alternatives exist. Communication may be extremely open among a group of women, and the demand for abortion may be high, but women will find it easy to reach the poorly qualified or expensive abortionist and impossible to reach others.

The following account is a striking example of the effects of inbreeding on the flow of information. The questionnaire was sent in by a young secretary from a suburb of New York. The woman was answering the question which asks for a description of how the abortionist was located.

> I asked several close college friends—all gave me the name and address of a doctor from their friends. From all, separately asked, I got the same name and address. My mother volunteered to help —she asked her friends who had any experience with it. They gave her the same name and address that I had gotten from my friends (one of them had been to him four times). All assured her that he was a competent doctor and abortionist. Before doing anything else, we went to see my family doctor—we have great faith in him—he told us he couldn't recommend anyone, or in any way become involved. However, when I gave him the name of the abortionist, he intimated, as discreetly as possible, that he knew who this was, and that he was competent.

Everyone this woman asked for help gave her the same address, and no one could give her any other addresses. In a highly inbred community in which communication about abortion is unusually open, she had no choice in which abortionist she reached.

*The Woman's Role within Her Acquaintance Universe: The Roles of "Girl" and "Woman"*

One of the central factors in different experiences is the social-sexual role which the woman assumes in her group. Married women are by definition sexually mature people. It may be embarrassing but it is not insulting to suggest to a married woman that sexually-related topics, like family planning, are relevant to her. The position with regard to unmarried women is less clear, and depends more on the woman's own definition of herself to other people. A teenage girl, for instance, is usually assumed by adults not to be sexually experienced unless there is some reason to think otherwise. An older unmarried woman, in her twenties or thirties, has considerable leeway in the image which she chooses to project of herself by her style of life, her place of residence, the subjects she initiates or avoids in conversation, and so forth.

It may be true that there is a considerable flow of information about abortion and people who have had abortions in an acquaintance universe, which may be offered to a woman if she gives the impression of being a person who would be interested in the subject and would not be offended or shocked. Or information may be withheld from her if she gives the impression, by the secrecy or discretion with which she conducts her private life, that she is not "eligible" to know about it or to contribute anything to the discussion. An example of this process of concealing information from others on the basis of a misunderstanding of the other's social-sexual role was mentioned by one woman, who took pains to withhold the knowledge of her abortion experience from a very close friend, because, she said, the girl friend was still a virgin as far as she knew and she didn't want to upset her or be misunderstood. When she had an opportunity to spend some time with this friend the next year, they discovered that each had been withholding knowledge of her sexual experience from the other, out of fear of shocking her.

### Perceived "Abortion Experts"

Women who live as sexually mature people and are unmarried, for example, career women who live alone away from their families and are not secretive about their relations with men, seem to be perceived by others as abortion experts, par excellence. Single and divorced women in their late twenties and thirties mentioned that they get frequent requests from married friends for help. One woman spoke of this at some length: she was actually anxious to help others in any way she could, but rather resented the assumption on the part of her "respectably" married friends and acquaintances that she would naturally know about a "sinful" thing like abortion. She felt that, although outwardly uncritical, others were expressing their envy and masked resentment at the freedom of her life by immediately thinking of her when the subject of abortion came up.

### Self-appointed "Abortion Specialists"

On the other hand, the self-appointed role of "abortion specialist" is an important aspect of understanding the distribution of information about abortion. Certain people, who may be men or women, let their friends and acquaintances know that they are knowledgeable about abortion. Some of these people are women who have had an abortion: others are just people who are sympathetic and feel that the situation is unjust. In the course of carrying out this study, about twenty such people outside the study group were located and we discussed their experience. Some refer only an occasional person to an abortionist, while others may receive as many as two or three requests for help per week over a period of months or years.

The word gets around that so-and-so is a good person to know if you need help with abortion, by the abortion specialist's own initiative in bringing the subject up with friends and by general gossip. The service of providing information, reassurance, and other help is not usually performed for money, although the recipient of help may send a gift and will almost surely be grateful for the help. The value of gifts received and the gratitude of people who are often not seen again does not entirely account for the motivation of a person who goes to a great deal of effort and a certain amount of risk to maintain a stock of information and make it available to others. There may be an element of vicarious participation in other people's crises involved. More important is the defiant, almost "civil disobedience" attitude of people who are ideologically committed to the position that abortion laws are unjust.

*Luck, Skill, and Persistence*

The women showed considerable personal variation in the resources which they brought to their search, aside from the structural sources of variation discussed. Some of the women located an abortionist quickly and easily, and did not have their personal qualities tested. Other women went to considerable lengths to track down leads, make a large number of fresh starts, and thoroughly explore all the possibilities. One woman, for instance, made appointments with eight different doctors located through the telephone book in the hope of finding one who would be willing to help her. Another asked thirty different friends for leads before locating an abortionist. No doubt there are some women who, when faced with the obstacles these women encountered, would have given up and resigned themselves to continuing the pregnancy.

In other cases, which would not appear by objective criteria to be any more promising in terms of the resources available for finding an abortionist, women had an easy time which can only be attributed to luck. One woman, for instance, had no friends or family in the area where she was living. When she suspected pregnancy, she went into the office of a doctor that she had noticed several times when she went past. The doctor confirmed the pregnancy and offered to perform a low-cost abortion for her. The Catholic woman who started crying in despair while at work was noticed by a distant acquaintance who stepped in and arranged her abortion. Another woman wrote to a number of friends in her distant home community. One of these wrote in turn to a friend in California, who in turn telephoned her sister, who happened to live near the pregnant girl. The sister came right over to the pregnant woman's apartment with a good address and an offer to lend money and drive her to the abortionist. These events can all be described as "one-in-a-thousand" chances, but when you are dealing with millions of events, you find that they are involved in a large number of cases.

In addition to luck and sheer persistence, women varied considerably in the extent to which they viewed their need to find an abortionist as an abstract problem. While abstract strategies were rare, they were striking in a few cases. One young nurse, for instance, deliberately initiated a conversation with a doctor over coffee about abortion. He mentioned the frequency with which he had seen women given approval for therapeutic abortions who had been exposed to the disease rubella (German measles). With this information in mind, the nurse called a friend who was assigned to the public health department of the city to ask to be allowed to expose herself to a patient with rubella. The strategy was abandoned when the public health nurse did not have any cases in her active case load. Another woman reported that she and her boyfriend figured out that the best place to pick up leads to a competent abortionist would be in an expensive hotel in Puerto Rico. They went to Puerto Rico for this purpose, but found it difficult to approach guests in such a hotel. The couple asked several taxi-drivers who served the hotel before locating an address from one of the women who worked in the hotel beauty shop. A third woman considered going to the "bohemian" section of town and just going up to nice-looking people in a coffee house, but did not carry out that plan. In general such strategies did not play a large role in making the actual arrangements, but are interesting for what they suggest about people's beliefs concerning sources of information and help.

Another aspect of personal persistence which played a role in the extent to which others were willing to help them arrange an abortion was not visible to the women themselves but was suggested by several of the "abortion specialists" that discussed their experiences. That factor is the degree of certainty or absence of ambivalence that the woman displayed in searching for an abortionist. Women who had already verified that they were pregnant and showed no hesitation in seeking abortion made it easiest for those they asked for help, while women who asked for help but also indicated that they were not certain they were pregnant, or were uncertain whether they should undergo abortion or go through with the pregnancy made it difficult for others to give out the addresses they had or commit themselves to help with abortion. One of the abortion specialists said that he always insists upon meeting the woman and talking personally with her about her problem. If she seemed to be partially inclined to get married or go through with the pregnancy in some other way, he would tell her that the doctor he knew of was on vacation and would not be back for six weeks. All three abortionists who volunteered to give information on their practice made similar statements under questioning, insisting that they would not terminate a pregnancy that was wanted by the mother, even if ambivalently, although one can imagine that in the course of a busy practice they might not actually ask the woman if she did not volunteer any information on her state of mind.

## Access to Legal Hospital Abortions

In order to get a legal abortion, it is usually necessary to have a long-standing relationship with a doctor as a private patient. It is not enough merely to have money to spend. The doctors who have connections with hospital abortion committees cannot be bribed to use their influence. They are most likely to be helpful to a woman they have known over a number of years, who is personally and socially the kind of woman they respect, and whom they know to be level-headed and unlikely either to embarrass the doctor by talking about it too much or to become hysterical or resentful afterward. A woman whose sexual behavior is beyond question or reproach will find it easiest to gain the cooperation of reputable physicians. A woman over forty is particularly likely to gain a sympathetic hearing, followed by younger mature women who have already had several children. A very young daughter of a highly respectable family will sometimes be favorably received, with the help of psychiatric testimony to support the family's case with discussions of "acting-out behavior" and "adolescent turmoil." The same girl who applied without the knowledge and support of her family would be very unlikely to succeed in obtaining permission.

Women who have a physician in their family or as a supportive friend are more likely to obtain a legal abortion than others. This is probably not due to the direct personal influence that such a doctor exercises over his colleagues who make the decision, but through the influence that he exercises over the applicants, indirectly or by deliberate coaching, in getting them to state their case in a way that is acceptable to the medical profession.

Only about one woman in a hundred can expect to obtain a hospital abortion under the current laws and the current medical interpretation of those laws. For those who do succeed, however, the advantages are considerable. Hospital abortions are performed under the best possible conditions from the point of view of safety, they usually do not require any travel, and the costs are reasonable and can often be paid by hospitalization insurance.

## Access to D. and C. Abortions Performed by a Physician with Anesthesia

The doctors who perform abortions with anesthesia tend to work in clinics rather than offices, tend to have assistants, tend to work on a full week schedule rather than confining abortions to weekends and evenings, and tend to have larger abortion practices than physicians who work without anesthesia. The information networks which lead to these abortionists tend to be large and far-flung. Women in the study group who obtained this type of abortion differed from others in the larger number of abortionists they learned about, suggesting that where women have a wide choice they choose an abortionist of this type, and in the longer distances they traveled to reach the abortionist. They did not noticeably differ from others in the number of persons they asked for help, the kinds of persons they asked, or in their social characteristics. As far as could be determined from the study group, it is very chancy whether a woman reaches this kind of abortionist or one of the less attractive types of specialist in abortion.

## Access to D. and C. Abortions Performed without Anesthesia

The most striking difference between women who got D. and C.

abortions with and without anesthesia is that the women who received no anesthesia were usually those who located only one abortionist. Since the abortionists were doctors, the women seemed to have accepted them as satisfactory and did not look further. These abortionists seem to be moderately successful physicians with a conventional practice, who do only an occasional abortion outside of office hours, usually with a considerable effort to maintain secrecy. There is a suggestion in the present study that when doctors give an address to a woman who comes to them for help that it is usually to one of these part-time abortionists rather than to one of the more professional abortionists.

## Access to Medically Untrained Abortionists

Among those in the study group who got catheter type abortions were professional women, students, nurses, clerical workers, and artists. Status differences in the allocation of types of abortions did not appear in the study group, probably because the differences were overridden by irrelevant elements such as the sources of referral to the study. In a large and systematically selected sample of cases of abortion, I would certainly expect to find that higher status women get abortions from physicians out of proportion to their numbers, and lower status women tend to obtain catheter abortions from nonphysicians.[7] One reason is that lower status women are less often able to pay the prices that physicians command, and an individual woman who is able to pay the higher costs may be blocked from access to a physician because her friends and acquaintances cannot afford doctors and have therefore never gained access to the information necessary to reach one. Medical abortionists may also practice a subtle form of class discrimination by deciding that they do not trust certain women who come to them, whose accents, clothes, or mannerisms may make the doctor uncomfortable and lead him to deny that he ever practices abortion.

The nonmedical abortionist, on the other hand, is probably more comfortable dealing with more disadvantaged women, who are less demanding than middle-class women. The nonmedical abortionist charges less and offers less than the physician. He usually does not maintain an office or special location for performing abortions.

[7]For a review of the socioeconomic differentials in access to legal and competent illegal abortions, see Edwin M. Schur, "Abortion," *The Annals of the American Academy of Political and Social Science* 376 (March 1968) : 136-47.

If he is conscientious he will try to avoid infection by being scrupulously clean, and may administer antibiotics to further reduce the risk of infection. At the least, he or she inserts a catheter and the task of emptying the uterus is left to the naturally occurring contractions. If infection sets in or if the process of abortion is complicated, the woman may have to go to the hospital for medical assistance. Because this possibility is more likely with a catheter abortion than with a D. and C., the nonmedical abortionist is more likely to be caught than the physician, and may protect himself from that possibility by being extremely secretive about his real identity, or conversely by trying to maintain a high level of solidarity with his patients.

The lower-class woman with the same personal qualities of skill, persistence, and absence of ambivalence as a middle-class woman, with the same number of friends willing to try to help and the same degree of openness of communication and lack of inbreeding in her acquaintance network may find that she can reach only an unskilled abortionist or a choice of several unskilled abortionists. On the other hand, the middle-class woman may have a better chance to reach a physician, but as we have seen it is entirely possible that with impressive amounts of resources and social skill she may yet "accidentally" be led to an unskilled abortionist.

### Access to Self-induced Abortions

One expert estimated that 80 percent of the women who are seen in hospital emergency wards from complications of illegal abortion have induced their own abortions with homemade equipment and vague knowledge.[8] No doubt this figure is somewhat inflated by women who claim to have done it themselves to protect others who were involved, but it is clear that self-induced abortions which are radical enough to terminate the pregnancy are very dangerous.

Only a few women in the study group had induced their own abortion, too few cases to be a basis for generalization. My guess is that there are subcultures in the society in which self-induced abortion is a common practice and the level of "folk-knowledge" of the practice, taught by one woman to another, is high enough to keep the level of danger reasonably low. Among the kinds of women who volunteered for this study, however, for whom essen-

[8]Calderone, *Abortion in the United States.*

tially all health matters and all births have been taken over by the medical profession and removed from public view into the hospitals, self-induced abortion is a desperately reckless act.

The women in the study group who induced their own abortions differed from others by being more isolated and less trustful that they would find a sympathetic reaction from others. They usually told the man involved about the pregnancy, but report that he did nothing to help them. One wonders whether the self-induced abortion was a gesture of anger toward him, or simply a result of inability to find an abortionist without his help. The women seemed to have in common a low valuation of their future reproductive capacity. Two of the women volunteered that they realized they were risking sterility by the abortion, but felt that it might be a blessing. Finally, these women seemed to have entertained the idea of death much more frequently than the women who sought a specialist in abortion, and did not find the idea entirely unattractive.

Women who were basically happy with themselves and their lives, no matter how upset they were over the unwanted pregnancy, could not bring themselves to use the catheters or douches that these women used to cause the abortion. The safe but ineffective techniques which were attempted by many of the women may have caused discomfort but they are within the normal range of stresses that the body is subjected to and do not require the same kind of determination and willingness to injure oneself that was shown by the women who actually induced their own abortions.

## Access to Abortion and Abortionists: Conclusion

We can specify some of the factors that are involved in leading some women to competent practitioners and others to incompetent and dangerous ones: an unconflicted desire for abortion, personal qualities of skill and persistence, access to money, and most of all, access to friends who are willing and able to help. In obtaining illegal abortion, to use the old cliché, it is not what you know but who you know that matters. It is not even true to say that any woman who makes the mistake or commits the sin of conceiving an unwanted pregnancy must take her chances with the available illegal abortionists. Instead, competent doctors make their services discreetly available to their middle-class patients, and the informal networks circulate this information among people similar in background, while poor women find only nonphysicians or self-induced methods available to them. Even two wealthy women of identical background with identical reasons for seeking abortion may find that while one is only temporarily inconvenienced by the unwanted pregnancy, the other must endure a difficult and humiliating search, fear, and despair in being forced to deal with unknown, inconsiderate abortionists, severe pain, and the risk of serious injury or even death. As long as abortion remains surreptitious and illegal and women still insist upon seeking abortion under some circumstances, it is difficult to see how the situation can be alleviated. Only under a system of legally provided abortion can decisions about abortion be made on universalistic grounds, and only when the decision lies entirely in the hands of the woman involved and the doctor she chooses can we be assured that incompetent abortionists will cease to practice.

*Appendix of Research Instruments*

# HARVARD UNIVERSITY
## DEPARTMENT OF SOCIAL RELATIONS

*William James Hall*
*Cambridge, Massachusetts 02138*
August 15, 1966

Miss Mary Jones
200 Main Street
City, State

Dear Miss Jones:

The Society for Humane Abortion in San Francisco tells me that you have an interest in their organization. In connection with a study of abortion, a number of people on the East Coast who are interested in the subject are being contacted, to ask for help in expanding the research.

I am conducting a study of how people make the arrangements to terminate a pregnancy, in the Department of Social Relations of Harvard University, under the supervision of sociologists and medical doctors. Information is being collected by questionnaires, from organizations like the Society for Humane Abortion, and from published accounts. The most important information must come, however, from interviews with a number of women who have actually had the experience of terminating a pregnancy. About twenty-five women, mostly in the Boston area, have volunteered and have been interviewed to date. The volunteers are asked to spend an hour or so describing their own experience. No names or addresses of any specific people are requested in the interview, and volunteers are carefully protected from identification. The final report of the study will consist of an analysis of approximately one hundred cases, in which no individuals will be identifiable.

You can increase the value of this research by helping to locate volunteers who are willing to talk about their experience. Perhaps you have friends, acquaintances or professional contacts who have frankly mentioned their experience to you. Would you contact any possible volunteers for the study, and ask them to write or phone me to arrange a meeting? Please do not send me a list of people you believe may be eligible for the study, without asking for their permission first, as we do not want anyone to feel that her confidence has been betrayed. Women of any age or marital status are eligible for the study, no matter how the termination of pregnancy was arranged. Each case is unique, and each makes a valuable contribution to the final result.

Interviews can be conducted in the volunteer's home or office, or in my office for those in the Boston area. To insure confidentiality, I am collecting all the interviews myself, so that even the research supervisors will not have access to the source of the interview. The contribution that you and the people you get in contact with can make to the study will be valuable in starting to understand this complex subject, and will be personally appreciated. Write me at the above address, or phone me in Boston at 491-4219 on Mondays or evenings. Please feel free to call collect.

Sincerely yours,

(Mrs.) Nancy Howell Lee

## RESEARCH QUESTIONNAIRE

The questionnaire on the following pages is for a study of the communication of information about birth control and abortion, and the experiences of people who have abortions. This questionnaire is only being given to a relatively small number of people who have indicated an interest in these subjects. Many of the questions are difficult to answer, and some may even be painful questions for a few people. Nevertheless, it is important to the success of the research to learn the attitudes and experiences of all those who are asked. I hope that you will take the fifteen minutes to an hour required to answer all the questions that apply to you.

Before you start, will you take a minute to read through the instructions on this page.

First of all, please do not fill out this questionnaire in public, where other people may read over your shoulder or notice how long it takes you to fill it out. The questions require some privacy and freedom from interruption to answer fully.

This questionnaire will be entirely confidential. There are no identifying marks anywhere on the questionnaire, and you should not write your own name or any other names anywhere on the form. Some of the questions, however, ask you to tell a little about some of the people you know. You may find it easier to make a list of their names on another sheet of paper and fill out the questionnaire form using that list, and then throw the list of names away. There will be no attempt to identify you or anyone else from the information you give here.

As you may know, every year a large number of women in this country have abortions. Some of these are legal and some are not. If you have ever had an abortion, please answer all the questions on the next eleven pages. If you have not had an abortion, just answer the questions on pages 2, 3 & 4, and then turn to the back cover, page 12, to complete the questionnaire.

All of the questions here can be answered quite briefly. If you would like to explain your attitudes or experiences in more detail, however, please feel free to write as much as you want and enclose it with the questionnaire. Your comments will be welcome and will be carefully studied.

The information gathered in this study will be used as the basis of a report, which will be available to social scientists, medical doctors, and others interested in the problems of birth control and abortion in America. I would like to express in advance my appreciation of your cooperation and interest in this research.

Return this questionnaire in the enclosed envelope to:

(Mrs.) Nancy Howell Lee
Sociology Section, Department of Social Relations
William James Hall 482
Harvard University
Cambridge, Mass. 02138

-2-

Part I.  Communication About Birth Control and Abortion

1.  Have you ever talked with the following people about how to keep from getting pregnant (birth control) or how to stop a pregnancy once it is started (abortion)?  Please circle your answer, yes or no, under the headings of "birth control" and "abortion."  If you don't know anyone in that category, circle "none."

| | Birth Control | | Abortion | |
|---|---|---|---|---|
| Your mother . . . . . . . . . None. . . | Yes | No | . . .Yes | No |
| Your sister . . . . . . . . . None. . . | Yes | No | . . .Yes | No |
| Your "best friend" . . . . . . . None. . . | Yes | No | . . .Yes | No |
| A neighbor . . . . . . . . . . None. . . | Yes | No | . . .Yes | No |
| Someone you work with . . . . None. . | Yes | No | . . .Yes | No |
| A friend who is not a neighbor . None. . . | Yes | No | . . .Yes | No |
| Your family doctor . . . . . . None. . . | Yes | No | . . .Yes | No |
| Your clergyman . . . . . . . None. . . | Yes | No | . . .Yes | No |
| A nurse . . . . . . . . . . . None. . . | Yes | No | . . .Yes | No |
| Your druggist . . . . . . . . None. . . | Yes | No | . . .Yes | No |

2.  Some people find that conversations about birth control make them uncomfortable or nervous, while others feel comfortable talking about it.  What about you, does talk about birth control make you uncomfortable?

_____

3.  Are there any particular people that you would not like to talk with about birth control?  If there are, tell who these people are (without mentioning any names) and why you would not like to talk with them.

_____

_____

_____

4.  Have you ever been in a conversation where abortion was discussed, such as how much it costs, how it is done, or how dangerous it is?_____

5.  Has anyone ever told you personally that she had an abortion?_____
If so, try to remember all the different people who have told you that they had an abortion, and tell what relationship these people have been to you (like "a woman I work with, " "my friend in school, " "my sister, " etc.).

_____

_____

_____

_____

6.  How many other women do you know who have had an abortion, even though you learned about it some other way?_____

-3-

7. According to what you have heard, how difficult do you think it is to get an abortion at the present time?_____

_____

What do you think it costs for most people?_____

Do you think it is likely to be dangerous to health or life?_____

_____

8. Have you talked with anyone about abortion in the past week?_____

9. Would you say that abortion is a common topic of conversation, or a rare one?_____

10. Are there any particular people that you would not want to talk with about abortion? If there are, tell who these people are, without mentioning any names, and why you would not like to talk with them.

_____

_____

_____

11. Imagine that you had some good reason for wanting to arrange for an abortion for yourself or for someone else. In the following lines, please describe what you would do to make the arrangements.

_____

_____

_____

_____

_____

12. Here is a list of some of the reasons that people might have for wanting to interrupt a pregnancy. If you think it is a good reason, and you would approve of their decision, circle "yes" after the reason. If you would not approve, just circle "no."

    If a married couple didn't want another child at that time . . . Yes   No
    If the pregnancy endangered the mother's health. . . . . . . Yes   No
    If the woman wasn't married . . . . . . . . . . . . . . . . Yes   No
    If the couple thinks they can not afford another child . . . . . Yes   No
    If the girl is under 16 years old . . . . . . . . . . . . . . Yes   No
    If the mother had taken drugs and the child might be deformed. Yes   No

13. In general, in what cases do you approve of abortions?_____

_____

14. In what cases do you disapprove of abortion, and think it should not be permitted?_____

_____

-4-

15. Has anyone ever come to you in the beginning of a pregnancy, to ask for help or advice about getting an abortion?_____ If so, please use the following space to describe briefly 1) the relationship to you of the person who asked for help, 2) why that person asked you, and 3) what you did about it.

_____

_____

_____

_____

Part II. Experience of Abortion

1. Have you personally ever ended a pregnancy by having an abortion?\_\_\_\_

> NOTE: If the answer to this question is No, turn to page 12 to complete the questionnaire. If you have ended one or more pregnancies by abortion, write the number of abortions you have had here, and answer the following questions for the first abortion you ever had.
> Number of abortions_____

2. In what month and year was the abortion performed?_____

3. At the time you first realized that you were pregnant, what was your age_____, your marital status_____, your occupation _____

4. How long after your first period was due did you realize that you were probably pregnant?_____

5. What was the first thing you did when you suspected that you were pregnant, did you tell someone about it, go to see a doctor, or something else?

_____

6. Did you decide to have an abortion immediately, or did you consider other alternatives?_____

7. Try to remember all the people you talked to when you were worried about being pregnant and trying to decide what to do. For each person that you talked to, please describe briefly who the person is, why you told that person, and what advice he or she gave you, if any. Do not include the people you just asked for help in arranging an abortion here. Do not use any names in your description.

_____

_____

_____

_____

_____

_____

_____

-5-

8. Did you talk with the man responsible for the pregnancy about the decision to have an abortion?_____

Did he agree that it was the best thing to do?_____
How active a part did he take in making the decision?_____

9. What kind of a relationship did you have with the man responsible for the pregnancy? (For example, was he your husband, your fiance, a close friend, a love relationship, a casual acquaintance, etc.)

_____

10. How long had you known the man when this pregnancy started?_____

11. How long had you two been having sexual relations?_____

12. Was he the first man you had sexual relations with?_____

13. Is there any question as to what man is responsible for the pregnancy?_____

14. What was the main reason for deciding to terminate the pregnancy?

_____

_____

15. Did you have a pregnancy test made?_____ If so, did you go to your regular doctor for the pregnancy test, a doctor that you had been to before? _____ (If not, how did you arrange to have the test made?)

_____

Was the doctor or the person who gave you the results of the test told that the pregnancy was unwanted?_____ Was he told that you were consider- ing an abortion?_____ If so, what was his or her reaction?_____

_____

16. The following is a list of methods of abortion that differ in safety and effectiveness. Check which methods you had heard of at the time of the abortion, which you considered using, and which methods you actually attempted to use.

|  | Heard of | Considered | Attempted |
|---|---|---|---|
| Getting a shot of progesterone . . . . . . | ____ | ____ | ____ |
| Unusual exercise or exertion . . . . . . | ____ | ____ | ____ |
| Hot or cold baths . . . . . . . . . . . . | ____ | ____ | ____ |
| Inserting a catheter or other object into the uterus. . . . . . . . . . . . | ____ | ____ | ____ |
| Taking drugs or home remedies . . . . . | ____ | ____ | ____ |
| A "therapeutic abortion" performed in a hospital. . . . . . . . . . . . . | ____ | ____ | ____ |
| An illegal operation. . . . . . . . . . . | ____ | ____ | ____ |
| Other _____ | ____ | ____ | ____ |

-6-

17. Think back now to all the people you asked for information on how to arrange an abortion, or for the address of an abortionist. Without mentioning any names, please describe briefly each person you asked for help, including 1) the relationship you had had with that person (such as a close friend, family doctor, sister, etc.), 2) the reason why you chose to ask that person, and 3) what help that person gave you (such as sending you to another person, asking around on your behalf, or actually giving you an address). This is a difficult question but an important one.

_____
_____
_____
_____
_____
_____
_____
_____
_____
_____
_____
_____
_____
_____
_____
_____
_____
_____
_____
_____
_____
_____
_____
_____

18.  If you got leads to more than one person who might perform an
abortion, summarize what you were told about each one.

1.  Qualifications (such as doctor, nurse, etc.)

_____

Method used (such as the methods mentioned in question 16)

_____

Cost of the abortion_____

Recommendation (Did you speak to someone who was actually able
to tell you whether the person is competent, such as a woman who
had already gone to him, or another doctor.)

_____

Did you try to contact this person?_____

If so, were you able to reach him or her?_____

2.  Qualifications_____

Method_____

Cost_____

Recommendation_____

Did you try to contact him?_____ Were you able to?_____

3.  Qualifications_____

Method_____

Cost_____

Recommendation_____

Did you try to contact him?_____ Were you able to?_____

4.  Qualifications_____

Method_____

Cost_____

Recommendation_____

Did you try to contact him?_____ Were you able to?_____

5.  Qualifications_____

Method_____

Cost_____

Recommendation_____

Did you try to contact him?_____ Were you able to?_____

19.  What was the most important factor in choosing to go to the person
you actually went to?_____

_____

20.  Which of the above people actually performed the abortion?_____

-8-

21. How far along was the pregnancy when you finally got in touch with the person who performed the abortion?_____

22. Did you see the abortionist for an examination and an interview before the abortion?_____

23. Were you given any medication before the abortion, like antibiotics or tranquilizers?_____ (Specify what it was if you know)_____

_____

24. Was it necessary to travel out of your local area to have the abortion ? _____ If so, about how far did you have to travel?_____

25. Was the abortionist located in a large city_____, a town _____, or a rural area_____?

26. Did you go for the abortion alone, or with someone else?_____ If you went with someone else, who was that?_____ If you went alone, did anyone know where you were that day?_____

27. In what setting was the abortion performed (for instance, a doctor's office, your home, a hotel, a hospital, etc.)?_____

28. Did the abortionist have any assistance?_____ If so, who did that person seem to be (a nurse, a doctor, etc.)?_____

29. Were there any other patients present when you had the abortion?____ If so, did they seem to be abortion patients too? _____

30. Were you given any anesthesia for the abortion?_____ (Specify the kind you were given if you know it)_____

31. Were you conscious during the abortion?_____ Were you in pain?____

32. How long did you rest afterward before going home or getting up and going about your usual business?_____

33. Were you given any antibiotics or other medication for after-care?____ (Specify type if known)_____

34. What was your impression of the abortionist? Did he (or she) seem like a pretty unpleasant person or a fairly decent person?_____

_____

35. All in all, were you satisfied by the way you were treated by the person who performed the abortion, or do you think you were treated badly?

_____

-9-

36. In the following lines, please fill in the costs of the various expenses associated with the abortion.

        Transportation _____
        Abortionist's Fee _____
        Medication _____
        Costs of after-care _____
        Other _____

37. If someone else helped you pay the costs, please indicate how much each person paid. _____

38. Was it necessary to borrow any money for the abortion expenses? _____
If so, please indicate the relationship to you of any people who lent money, and whether they were told of the pregnancy.

_____
_____

39. Did you have any of the following symptoms after the abortion? If so, please indicate how severely you had the symptom, and how long it lasted.

    Excessive bleeding_____
    Pain _____
    General Weakness_____
    Fever _____
    Depression_____
    Nightmares_____
    Cramps _____
    Other (please specify)_____

40. Were you hospitalized for any reason related to the abortion? _____
If so, please explain why. _____

_____

41. Did you go to a doctor for treatment or for a check-up after the abortion?
_____ Was this your regular doctor, or did you get a new doctor?_____
Did you tell this doctor that you had had an abortion?_____ Did you discuss contraception with him at that time? _____

42. Going back to the time that the pregnancy started, would you say you were using contraception regularly_____, usually _____, occasionally_____, or not at all____.

43. If you were using contraception at that time, what kind or method were you using?_____
How do you think the pregnancy occurred? Did you skip contraception once or more_____, did you use the contraceptive carelessly _____, or did it just fail to work____?

44. Have you started using contraception or changed your method since the abortion?_____ If so, what method are you now using?_____

-10-

45. Would you say that your relationship with the man responsible for the pregnancy improved____, remained the same____, or got worse____ during the time of the pregnancy and the abortion?

46. Did you break up, or separate, at that time?_____ If so, do you think that would have happened anyway, even if the pregnancy had not occurred?_____

47. Have you changed your marital status since the time of the pregnancy? _____ If you married since that time, did you marry the man responsible for the pregnancy discussed here?_____

If you have married someone else, did you ever tell your husband about the abortion?_____

48. Think now of all of the people that you have told that you had an abortion since it happened. Include anyone that you told in detail and those you just mentioned it to, but do not include the people that you already described in questions 7 and 17. In the following lines, briefly describe the relationship to you of all the people you have told that you can remember. Be sure to include any doctors you have told for medical reasons.

_____

_____

_____

_____

_____

_____

_____

If you have told so many people that you can't remember them all, just make a guess as to how many people that might be. _____

49. Are there any people that you are particularly anxious should not find out about your experience, like your parents, your children, or your employer or family doctor?_____ If so, who are they?_____

_____

50. Since the abortion, you may have passed on the address of the person who performed the abortion for you to other people. Has anyone directly asked you for the address, who knew that you had an abortion?_____ Have you volunteered the address to anyone who needed it, who did not know about your experience?_____

51. How many people, all together, have you given the address to?_____

52. Would you go out of your way to help a person you didn't know very well to find an abortionist?_____

53. Would you report the fact of your abortion on a routine medical history form, if you were asked?_____

-11-

54. If you have had more than one abortion, please answer the following brief questions about your later experience. If you had only one abortion, please go on to question 55 on this page.

Second Abortion Experience

1. How many years and months passed between the first and second abortion?
_____
2. Did you immediately decide to have an abortion? _____
3. Was the same man responsible for this pregnancy as the first one? _____
4. What method of contraception were you using at that time? _____
5. How do you think this pregnancy occurred? _____
6. Roughly how many people did you tell of the pregnancy before it was terminated? _____
7. Did you return to the same person for an abortion? _____
   If not, was that because the person was no longer available? _____
8. How many addresses of people who would perform an abortion did you collect, that you did not have the first time? _____
9. What was the cost of the abortion? _____
10. Did you have any difficulty or complications from the abortion? _____
    Were you hospitalized for any reason related to the abortion? _____
11. Did you break up or separate from the man responsible for the pregnancy at that time? _____
12. Roughly how many people have you told of this abortion since it occurred? _____

Third Abortion Experience

1. How many years and months passed between the second and third abortion? _____
2. Did you immediately decide to have an abortion? _____
3. Was the same man responsible for this pregnancy as in the second one? _____
4. What method of contraception were you using at that time? _____
5. How do you think this pregnancy occurred? _____
6. Roughly how many people did you tell of the pregnancy before it was terminated? _____
7. Did you return to the same person for an abortion as in the second one? _____ If not, was that because the person was no longer available? _____
8. How many addresses of people who would perform an abortion did you collect, that you did not have the second time? _____
9. What was the cost of the abortion? _____
10. Did you have any difficulty or complications from the abortion? _____
    Were you hospitalized for any reason related to the abortion? _____
11. Did you break up or separate from the man responsible for the pregnancy at that time? _____
12. Roughly how many people have you told of this abortion since it occurred? _____

55. Have your feelings or attitudes about abortion changed in any way due to your experience? How do you now feel about abortion?

_____

_____

Thank you for your frankness. Please complete the questionnaire by answering the background questions on page 12.

-12-

Part III. Background Questions

1. Your age_____ Current marital status _____

2. Your religious affiliation _____ Are you an active member of a church or synagogue?_____

3. Your occupation (please be specific)_____

4. What is the highest grade of school or college you completed?_____
How old were you when you finished your formal education?_____

5. How old were you when it first became possible for you to become pregnant, counting from the time of your first marriage or first sexual experience?_____

6. Was there any time in your life prior to your marriage (if any) when you lived away from your parental family?_____ If so, please indicate how old you were when that period started and how old you were when it ended, if it has ended. _____

7. How many times altogether have you been pregnant, counting any babies you have had and any miscarriages or abortions?_____
In the following lines, please indicate your age at the time of each pregnancy and the type of termination that occurred (by live birth, miscarriage, abortion or stillbirth).

| Your Age | Type of Termination of Pregnancy | Your marital status at that time |
|---|---|---|
|  |  |  |
|  |  |  |
|  |  |  |
|  |  |  |
|  |  |  |

8. Have you ever used any methods of birth control to prevent pregnancy?
_____ If so, how successful have you been in using birth control to regulate the number and spacing of your pregnancies?_____

9. In the following space, please fill in the age, sex, and relationship to you of all the people who live in your household.

| Your Age | Sex | Relationship to you (such as husband, child, friend) |
|---|---|---|
|  |  |  |
|  |  |  |
|  |  |  |
|  |  |  |

10. Without mentioning any names, please tell how you got this questionnaire.

Thank you for your help. Please return this questionnaire in the enclosed envelope, which needs no postage.

# Bibliography

## Part 1. On Abortion

Amen, J. H. "Some Obstacles to Effective Legal Control of Criminal Abortion." In National Committee on Maternal Health, *The Abortion Problem*. Baltimore: Williams & Wilkins Co., 1944, pp. 134-42.

Aptekar, Herbert. *Infanticide, Contraception and Abortion in Savage Society*. New York: Wm. Godwin, 1931.

Aren, Per. "Legal Abortion in Sweden." *Acta Obstetrica et Gynecologica Scandanavica*, vol. 36, supplement 1, 1958.

Ball, Donald W. "An Abortion Clinic Ethnography." *Social Problems* 14 (Winter 1967) : 293-301.

Bates, Jerome E. "The Abortion Mill: An Institutional Analysis." *Journal of Criminal Law, Criminology and Police Science* 45 (July–August 1954) : 163.

Bates, Jerome E., and Zawadzki, Edward S. *Criminal Abortion*. Springfield, Ill.: Thomas, 1964.

Bolter, Sidney. "The Psychiatrist's Role in Therapeutic Abortion: The

Unwitting Accomplice." *American Journal of Psychiatry* 119 (October 1962) : 312-16.

_____. "Ethics and Abortion." *Journal of the American Medical Association* 180 (June 1962) : 29.

Brunner, Endre K. "The Outcome of 1556 Conceptions, a Medical-Sociologic Study." *Human Biology* 13 (1941) : 159-76.

Brunner, Endre K., and Newton, L. "Abortions in Relation to Viable Births in 10,609 Pregnancies." *American Journal of Obstetrics and Gynecology* 38 (1939) : 82-90.

Browne, Stella. "The Right of Abortion." *Journal of Sex Education* 5 (1952) : 29-32.

Browne, Stella; Ludovici, A. M.; and Roberts, H. *Abortion.* London: Geo. Allen & Unwin, Ltd., 1935.

Calderone, Mary S., ed. *Abortion in the United States.* Proceedings of the conference held under the auspices of Planned Parenthood Federation of America in April and June, 1955. New York: Hoeber Harper, 1958.

Caplan, Gerald. "Disturbance of the Mother-Child Relationship by Unsuccessful Attempts at Abortion." *Mental Hygiene* 38 (1954) : 67.

Collins, J. H. "Abortions—a Study Based on 1,304 Cases." *American Journal of Obstetrics and Gynecology* 62 (1951) : 548-58.

Devereaux, George. *A Study of Abortion in Primitive Societies.* New York: Julian Press, 1955.

Ekblad, Martin. "Induced Abortion on Psychiatric Grounds: A Follow-up Study of 479 Women." Trans. D. Burton. *Acta Psychiatrica et Neurologica Scandinavica,* Supplement 99. Stockholm, 1955.

Eliasberg, Wladimir G. "Psychiatry in Prenatal Care and the Problem of Abortion." *Medical Woman's Journal* 58 (1951) : 27-31.

Engle, Earl T., ed. *Pregnancy Wastage.* Proceedings of a conference sponsored by the Committee on Human Reproduction, National Research Council, in behalf of the Committee on Maternal Health, Inc. Springfield, Ill.: Thomas, 1953.

Ferris, Paul. *The Nameless: Abortion in Britain Today.* London: Hutchinson, 1966.

Fisher, Russell S. "Criminal Abortion." *Journal of Criminal Law and Criminology* 42 (July–August 1951) : 242-49.

Freeman, Lucy. *The Abortionist* (By Dr. X as told to Lucy Freeman.) London: Victor Gollancz, Ltd., 1962.

Gebhard, Paul H., *et al. Pregnancy, Birth and Abortion.* New York: Harper & Bros. and Paul H. Hoeber, Inc., 1958.

Guttmacher, Alan F. "Therapeutic Abortion: Doctor's Dilemma." *Journal of Mt. Sinai Hospital* 21 (1954) : 111.

_____. "The Shrinking Non-Psychiatric Indications for Therapeutic Abortion." In *Therapeutic Abortion: Medical, Psychiatric, Legal, Anthropological and Religious Considerations,* ed. Harold Rosen, pp. 12-21. New York: Julian Press, 1954.

Hall, William E. "Some Signs, Findings and Interpretations of Criminal Abortion." *Journal of Criminal Law and Criminology* 41 (July–August 1950) : 235-43.

Hamilton, Virginia C. "Some Observations on the Contraceptive Behavior of Abortion Patients." *Human Fertility* 6 (1941) : 37-41.

_____. "Some Sociologic and Psychologic Observations on Abortion." *American Journal of Obstetrics and Gynecology* 39 (1940) : 91-128.

Hooh, Kertin. "Refused Abortion." *Acta Psychiatrica Scandinavica* 39 (supplement 168, 1963) : 1-156.

Javert, Carl T. *Spontaneous and Habitual Abortion.* New York: Blakiston, 1957.

Klinger, Andras. "Abortion Programs." In *Family Planning and Population Programs,* ed Berelson *et al.,* pp. 465-76. Chicago: University of Chicago Press, 1965.

Koguchi, Yasuaki. "The Prevalence of Induced Abortion in Present Day Japan." In *Report of the Proceedings of the Fifth International Conference on Planned Parenthood.* London: International Planned Parenthood Association, 1955.

Kolstad, Per. "Therapeutic Abortion." *Acta Obstetricia et Gynecologica Scandinavica,* vol. 36, supplement 6, 1957.

Koya, Yoshio. "A Study of Induced Abortion in Japan and Its Significance." *Milbank Memorial Fund Quarterly* 32 (1954) : 282-93.

Kummer, Jerome M. "Post-Abortion Psychiatric Illness—A Myth?" *American Journal of Psychiatry* 119 (April 1963) : 983.

_____. "Psychiatric Contra-indications to Pregnancy." *California Medicine* 79 (July 1953) : 31-35.

Kummer, Jerome M., and Leavy, Zad. "Therapeutic Abortion Law Confusion." *Journal of the American Medical Association* 195 (January 10, 1966) : 96-100.

Lader, Lawrence. *Abortion.* Indianapolis: Bobbs Merrill Co., 1966.

Mehlan, K. H. "The Effects of Legalization of Abortion." *Proceedings of the Third Conference of the Region for Europe, Near East and Africa of the International Planned Parenthood Federation,* 1962, pp. 209-19.

————. "The Effects of Legalization of Abortion on the Health of Mothers in Eastern Europe." *Proceedings of the Seventh International Conference on Planned Parenthood,* 1963, pp. 214-22.

————. "Family Planning in the East European Socialist Countries." In *Family Planning Programs—Proceedings of an International Conference, August, 1965.* Chicago: University of Chicago Press, 1966.

Merle, Beatrice B. "An Analysis of Abortion Deaths in the District of Columbia for the Years 1938, '39, and '40." *American Journal of Obstetrics and Gynecology* 59 (1947) : 321.

Mumford, R. S. "An Interdisciplinary Study of Four Wives Who Had Induced Abortions." *American Journal of Obstetrics and Gynecology* 87 (December 1963) : 865-76.

National Committee on Maternal Health. *The Abortion Problem.* Proceedings of the 1942 Conference on Maternal Health, 1944.

Newman, Lucile. "Abortion as Folk Medicine." *California Health,* October–November 1965, pp. 75–79.

Packer, Herbert L., and Campbell, Ralph J. "Therapeutic Abortion: A Problem in Law and Medicine." *Stanford Law Review* 11 (May 1959) : 418-19.

Pollak, Otto. *The Criminality of Women.* Philadelphia: University of Pennsylvania Press, 1950.

Rosen, Harold, ed. *Therapeutic Abortion.* New York: Julian Press, Inc., 1954.

Rossi, Alice S. "Abortion Laws and Their Victims." *Trans-action,* November, 1966.

————. "Public Views on Abortion." Unpublished paper, Committee on Human Development, University of Chicago, February 1966.

Schur, Edwin M. "Abortion." *The Annals of the American Academy of Political and Social Science* 376 (March 1968) : 136-47.

————. "Abortion and the Social System." *Social Problems,* October 1955, pp. 94-99.

————. *Crimes without Victims: Abortion, Homosexuality, Drug Addiction.* Englewood Cliffs, N.J.: Prentice-Hall, 1965.

Simons, J. H. "Statistical Analysis of One Thousand Abortions."

*American Journal of Obstetrics and Gynecology* 37 (1939): 840-49.

Stix, Regina K. "A Study of Pregnancy Wastage." *Milbank Memorial Fund Quarterly* 13 (September 1938): 621-29.

"Symposium on the Social Problem of Abortion." *Bulletin of the Sloane Hospital for Women,* vol. 7, Fall 1965.

Taussig, Frederick J. "Abortion and Its Relation to Fetal and Maternal Mortality." *American Journal of Obstetrics and Gynecology* 33 (1937): 711-14.

_____. "Abortion Control through Birth Control." In *Medical and Biological Aspects of Contraception,* pp. 61-70. National Committee on Federal Legislation for Birth Control, 1934.

_____. "Abortion in Relation to Fetal and Maternal Welfare." In *Fetal Newborn and Maternal Morbidity and Mortality,* White House Conference on Child Health and Protection, pp. 449-93. New York: D. Appleton-Century Co., 1933.

_____. "The Abortion Problem in Russia." *American Journal of Obstetrics and Gynecology* 22 (1931): 134-39.

_____. *Abortion, Spontaneous and Induced: Medical and Social Aspects.* St. Louis: C. V. Mosby Co., 1936.

Tietze, Christopher. "Abortion as a Cause of Death." *American Journal of Public Health,* vol. 38, no. 2 (October, 1948).

_____. "Introduction to the Statistics of Abortion." In *Pregnancy Wastage,* ed. Engle. Springfield: Thomas, 1953.

_____. "The Demographic Significance of Legal Abortion in Eastern Europe." *Demography* 1 (1964): 119-25.

_____. "Induced Abortion and Sterilization as Methods of Fertility Control." *Journal of Chronic Diseases* 18 (1965): 1161-71; and Publication no. 27, National Committee on Maternal Health, New York.

_____. "An Investigation into the Incidence of Abortion in Baltimore." *American Journal of Obstetrics and Gynecology,* October–December 1959.

_____. "Some Facts about Legal Abortion." In Roy O. Greep, *Human Fertility and Population Problems.* Cambridge: Schenkman Publishing Co., 1963.

Tietze, Christopher, and Lehfeldt, Hans. "Legal Abortion in Eastern Europe," *Journal of the American Medical Association* 175 (April 1, 1961): 1149-54.

Tietze, Christopher, and Martin, Clyde E. "Foetal Deaths, Spontaneous and Induced, in the Urban White Population of the U.S." *Population Studies* 11 (1957) : 170-76.

Watkins, R. E. "A Five Year Study of Abortion." *American Journal of Obstetrics and Gynecology*, vol. 26, 1933.

Whelpton, P. K. "Frequency of Abortion: Its Effects on the Birth Rates and Future Population of America." *The Abortion Problem.* Proceedings of the 1942 Conference on Maternal Health, 1944, pp. 14-26.

Wiehl, Dorothy. "A Summary of Data on Reported Incidence of Abortion." *Milbank Memorial Fund Quarterly* 16 (January, 1938): 219-27.

Williams, Glanville. *The Sanctity of Life and the Criminal Law.* New York: Alfred A. Knopf, 1957.

Woodside, Moya. "Attitudes of Women Abortionists." *Family Planning*, vol. 12, no. 2 (July, 1963).

## Part 2   On Networks and Communication

Allport, Gordon W., and Postman, L. *The Psychology of Rumor.* New York: Henry Holt, 1947.

Bach, Kurt, *et al.* "A Method of Studying Rumor Transmission." In *Theory and Experiment in Social Communication*, ed. L. Festinger, pp. 307-12. Research Center for Group Dynamics, University of Michigan, 1950.

Berelson, Bernard R. "Communication, Communication Research, and Family Planning." In *Emerging Techniques in Population Research*, pp. 159-71. New York: Milbank Memorial Fund, 1963.
——————. "On Family Planning Communication." *Demography* 1 (1964) : 94-105.

Berelson, Bernard R., Lazarsfeld, Paul F.; and McPhee, William N. *Voting: A Study of Opinion Formation in a Presidential Campaign.* Chicago: University of Chicago Press, 1954.

Bott, Elizabeth. *Family and Social Network.* London: Tavistock Publications, 1957.

Coleman, James; Katz, Elihu; and Menzel, Herbert. "The Diffusion of an Innovation among Physicians." *Sociometry* 20 (December, 1957) : 253-70.

Cowles, Wylda, and Polgar, Steven. "Health and Communication in a Negro Census Tract." *Social Problems*, vol. 10, no. 3 (Winter 1963).

Dodd, Stuart C. "Diffusion Is Predictable." *American Sociological Review* 20 (1955) : 392-401.

————. "A Test of Message Diffusion by Chain Tags." *American Journal of Sociology* 61 (1956) : 425-32.

————. "Testing Message Diffusion in Controlled Experiments: Charting the Distance and Time Factors in the Interactance Hypothesis." *American Sociological Review*, vol. 18, no. 4 (August 1953).

Festinger, L., *et al.* "A Study of a Rumor: Its Origin and Spread." *Human Relations* 1 (1948) : 464-86.

Gurevitch, Michael. *The Social Structure of Acquaintance Networks.* Ph.D. diss., Massachusetts Institute of Technology, June 1961.

Harary, Frank; Norman, Robert Z.; and Cartwright, Dorwin. *Structural Models: An Introduction to the Theory of Directed Graphs.* New York: John Wiley & Sons, 1965.

Katz, Elihu. "The Two-Step Flow of Communication: An Up-to-Date Report on an Hypothesis." *Public Opinion Quarterly* 21 (Spring 1957) : 61-78.

Katz, Elihu; Hamilton, Herbert; and Levin, Martin L. "Traditions of Research on the Diffusion of Innovation." *American Sociological Review* 28 (1963) : 237-52.

Katz, Elihu, and Lazarsfeld, Paul. *Personal Influence.* Glencoe, Ill.: The Free Press, 1955.

Kecshemeti, Paul. "Totalitarian Communication as a Means of Control." *Public Opinion Quarterly* 19 (Summer 1950) : 224-34.

Lazarsfeld, Paul; Berelson, Bernard; and Gaudet, Hazel. *The People's Choice.* New York: Columbia University Press, 1948.

Merton, Robert K. "Patterns of Influence: A Study of Interpersonal Influence and Communications Behavior in a Local Community." In *Communication Research 1948-49*, ed. Paul F. Lazarsfeld and Frank N. Stanton, pp. 180-219. New York: Harper and Brothers, 1949.

Moreno, Jacob L. *Who Shall Survive?* New York: Beacon Press, 1953.

Mullins, Nicholas. *Social Foundations of Informal Communication in the Biological Sciences.* Ph.D. diss., Harvard University, 1966.

Orjar, Oyen, and Defleur, Melvin L. "The Spacial Diffusion of an Airborne Leaflet Message." *American Journal of Sociology* 59 (September 1953) : 144-49.

Ore, Oystein. *Graphs and Their Uses.* New York: Random House, 1963.

Pool, Ithiel, *et al.* "A Non-Mathematical Introduction to a Mathematical Model"; "Mathematical Models for Social Contact"; "Contact Nets"; "The Collection of Contact Net Data"; "Notes on the Empirical Results of the Project." Unpublished papers, Massachusetts Institute of Technology, 1966.

Rapoport, Anatol. "Mathematical Models of Social Interaction." In *Handbook of Mathematical Psychology,* ed. Luce, Bush, and Galanter, vol. 2. New York: John Wiley & Sons, 1963.

Ryan, Bryce, and Gross, Neal. "The Diffusion of Hybrid Seed Corn in Two Iowa Communities." *Rural Sociology* 8 (1942) : 15-24.

Shils, Edward A. "The Study of the Primary Group." In *The Policy Sciences,* ed. Daniel Lerner and Harold Lasswell. Stanford: Stanford University Press, 1951.

## Part 3. **On Reproductive Behavior: Fertility, Contraception, Illegitimacy, and Premarital Sexual Relations**

Aberle, Sophie D., and Corner, George W. *Twenty-five Years of Sex Research: History of the National Research Council Committee for Research in Problems of Sex, 1922-1947.* Philadelphia: W. B. Saunders Co., 1953.

Adams, Hannah M., and Gallagher, Ursula M. "Some Facts and Observations about Illegitimacy." *Children* 10 (March–April 1964) : 43-48.

Bakker, C. B., and Dightman, C. R. "Physicians and Family Planning—A Persistent Ambivalence." *Obstetrics and Gynecology* 25 (February 1965) : 279-84.

Ball, John C., and Logan, Nell. "Early Sexual Behavior of Lower Class Delinquent Girls." *Journal of Criminal Law and Criminology* 51 (July–August 1960) : 209-14.

Berelson, Bernard. "Sample Surveys and Population Control." *Public Opinion Quarterly* 28 (Fall 1964) : 361-94.

Berelson Bernard, *et al.,* eds. *Family Planning and Population Programs.* Chicago: University of Chicago Press, 1965.

Boek, Walter E., *et al. Social Class, Maternal Health and Child Care.* Albany, N.Y.: State Department of Health, 1957.

Borgatta, E. F., and Westoff, C. F. "The Prediction of Total Fertility."

*Milbank Memorial Fund Quarterly* 32 (October 1954) : 383-419.

Bromley, Dorothy D., and Britten, Florence H. *Youth and Sex: A Study of 1300 College Students.* New York: Harper & Bros., 1938.

Calderone, Mary S., ed. *Manual of Contraceptive Practice.* Baltimore: Williams & Wilkins, 1964.

Campbell, Arthur A. "Incidence of Operations That Prevent Conceptions." *American Journal of Obstetrics and Gynecology* 89 (July 1964) : 694-709.

Chambliss, Rollin. "Contributions of the Vital Statistics of Finland to the Study of Factors that Induce Marriage." *American Sociological Review* 18 (February 1957) : 38-48.

Christensen, H. T. "Cultural Relativism and Premarital Sex Norms." *American Sociological Review* 25 (February 1960) : 31-39.

Christensen, H. T., and Meissner, H. H. "Studies in Child Spacing: Pre-marital Pregnancy as a Factor in Divorce." *American Sociological Review* 18: 641-44.

Clemmensen, Carl. "State of Legal Abortion in Denmark." *American Journal of Psychiatry* 112 (1956) : 662-63.

Cloward, Richard A. "Illegitimate Means, Anomie, and Deviant Behavior." *American Sociological Review* 24 (April 1959) : 164-76.

Cutright, Phillips, and Galle, Omer. "Illegitimacy: Measurement and Analysis." Unpublished paper, Vanderbilt University, Department of Sociology, November 1966.

Davis, Katherine B. *Factors in the Sex Life of 2200 Women.* New York: Harper & Bros., 1929.

Davis, Kinsley. "Illegitimacy and the Social Structure." *American Journal of Sociology* 45 (1939) : 215-33.

Davis, Kinsley, and Blake, Judith. "Social Structure and Fertility: An Analytic Framework." *Economic Development and Cultural Change* 4 (1956) : 211-35.

Ford, Clelland S., and Beach, Frank A. *Patterns of Sexual Behavior.* New York: Harper & Bros., 1951.

Freedman, Ronald. "The Sociology of Human Fertility." *Current Sociology*, 1961-62, pp. 35-121.

Freedman, Ronald and Coombs, Lolagene. "Childspacing and Family Economic Position." *American Sociological Review* 31 (October 1966) : 631-48.

————. "Economic Considerations in Family Growth Decisions." *Population Studies,* vol. 20, 1966.

Freedman, Ronald; Whelpton, P. K.; and Campbell, A. A. *Family Planning, Sterility and Population Growth.* New York: McGraw Hill, 1959.

Greep, Roy O., ed. *Human Fertility and Population Problems.* Cambridge, Mass.: Schenkman Publishing Co., 1963.

Guttmacher, Alan F. "Conception Control and the Medical Profession: The Attitude of 3,381 Physicians toward Contraception and the Contraceptives They Prescribe." *Human Fertility* 12 (March 1947): 1-10.

————. "Miscarriages and Abortions." In *Successful Marriage,* ed. M. Fishbein and E. Burgess. Garden City: Doubleday, 1947.

————. "The United States Medical Profession and Family Planning." In *Family Planning and Population Programs,* ed. Berelson *et al.* Chicago: University of Chicago Press, 1965.

Hall, Oswald. "Sociological Research in the Field of Medicine." *American Sociological Review* 16 (1951): 639-44.

Hall, Robert E. "Therapeutic Abortion, Sterilization and Contraception." *American Journal of Obstetrics and Gynecology* 91 (February 15, 1965): 518-32.

Handel, G., and Rainwater, L. "Working-class People and Family Planning. *Social Work* 6 (April 1961): 18-25.

Heer, David M. "Abortion, Contraception and Population Policy in the Soviet Union." *Demography,* vol. 2, June 1965.

Herzog, Elizabeth. "Unmarried Mothers." *Child Welfare,* October 1962, p. 342.

Hill, R.; Stycos, J. M.; and Bach, K. W. *The Family and Population Control.* Chapel Hill: University of North Carolina Press, 1959.

Jerome, Himelock, and Fava, Sylvia F. *Sexual Behavior in American Society.* New York: W. W. Norton, 1955.

Himes, Norman E. *Medical History of Contraception.* Baltimore: Williams & Wilkins, 1936.

Hoffmeyer, H. "Psychological Resistance against Contraception." *Proceedings of the Second Conference of the Region for Europe, Near East and Africa.* International Planned Parenthood Federation, 1960, pp. 105-8.

Hollingworth, Leta S. "Social Devices for Compelling Women to Bear and Rear Children." *American Journal of Sociology* 22 (July 1916): 28-29.

Hughes, Everett C. "The Making of a Physician: General Statement of Ideas and Problems." *Human Organization* 14 (1956): 21-23.

Kinsey, Alfred C., *et al. Sexual Behavior in the Human Female.* Philadelphia: W. B. Saunders Co., 1953.

Kiser, C. V., and Whelpton, P. K. "Resumé of the Indianapolis Study of Social and Psychological Factors Affecting Fertility." *Population Studies* 7 (November 1953): 95-110.

Lafitte, F. "The Users of Birth Control Clinics." *Population Studies* 16 (July 1962): 12-30.

Lee, Alfred M. "The Social Dynamics of the Physician's Status." *Psychiatry* 7 (1944): pp. 371-77.

Lehfeldt, H. "Willful Exposure to Unwanted Pregnancy: Psychological Explanations for Patient Failures in Contraception." *In Sixth International Conference on Planned Parenthood,* pp. 110-14, 1959. Also in *American Journal of Obstetrics and Gynecology* 78 (September 1959): pp. 661-65.

Mauldin, W. P. "Fertility Studies: Knowledge, Attitude and Practice." *Studies in Family Planning* 7 (June 1965): 1-10.

Meier, Richard L. *Modern Science and the Human Fertility Problem.* New York: John Wiley & Sons, 1959.

Mills, C. A., and Ogle, Cordelia. "Physiologic Sterility of Adolescence." *Human Biology* 8 (1936): 607-715.

Monahan, T. P. "Premarital Pregnancy in the United States." *Eugenics Quarterly,* 1960.

Montagu, F. A. Ashley. *The Reproductive Development of the Female.* New York: Julian Press, 1957.

Noonan, John T., Jr. *Contraception.* Cambridge, Mass.: Harvard University Press, 1965.

Notestein, Frank W., and Kiser, Clyde V. "Factors Affecting Variations in Human Fertility." *Social Forces* 14 (1935): 32-41.

Pearl, Raymond. "Fertility and Contraception in New York and Chicago." *Journal of the American Medical Association* 108 (1937): 1394.

Perrin, Edward B., and Sheps, Mindel C. "Human Reproduction: A Stochastic Process." *Biometrics* 20 (March 1964): 28-45.

————. "A Mathematical Model for Human Fertility Patterns." *Archives of Environmental Health* 10 (May 1965): 694-98.

Polgar, Steven. "Social Science Research in Planned Parenthood Centers." In *Advances in Planned Parenthood,* ed. A. J. Sobrero and S. Lewit. Cambridge, Mass.: Schenkman Publishing Co., 1965.

Potter, Robert G. "Length of the Fertile Period." *Milbank Memorial Fund Quarterly* 39 (January 1961): 132-62.

_____. "Some Comments on the Evidence Pertaining to Family Limitations in the United States." *Population Studies* 14 (July 1960): 40-54.

_____. "Some Problems in Predicting a Couple's Contraceptive Future." *Eugenics Quarterly* 6 (December 1959): 254-59.

_____. "Some Relationships between Short Range and Long Range Risks of Unwanted Pregnancy." *Milbank Memorial Fund Quarterly* 38 (July 1960): 255-63.

Potter, Robert G., and Kantner, J. F. "The Influence of Siblings and Friends on Fertility," *Milbank Memorial Fund Quarterly* 33 (July 1955): 246-67.

Potter, Robert G., and Parker, M. P. "Predicting the Time Required to Conceive." *Population Studies* 18 (July 1964): 99.

Pratt, William F. "Pre-marital Pregnancies and Illegitimate Births in a Metropolitan Community—An Analysis of Age and Color Differentials." Unpublished paper, delivered at the meetings of the Population Association of America, April 1965.

Rains, Prue. "Unmarried Pregnancy as a Focus of Social and Personal Reactions." Ph.D. diss. proposal, Northwestern University, Spring 1966.

Rainwater, Lee. *Family Design: Marital Sexuality, Family Size and Contraception.* Chicago: Aldine, 1965.

Rainwater, Lee, and Weinstein, Karol. "And the Poor Get Children." In *Sex, Contraception and Family Planning in the Working Class.* Chicago: Quadrangle Books, 1960.

Regan, Louis J. *Doctor and Patient and the Law.* St. Louis: C. V. Mosby Co., 1954.

Reiss, Ira L. "Class and Premarital Sexual Permissiveness." *American Sociological Review,* October 1965, pp. 747–56.

_____. "Premarital Sexual Permissiveness among Negroes and Whites." *American Sociological Review,* 29 (October, 1964): 688-98.

_____. *Premarital Sexual Standards in America.* New York: The Free Press, 1960.

_____. "The Sexual Renaissance." *The Journal of Social Issues,* vol. 22, 1966.

Ridley, Jeanne C., and Sheps, Mindel C. "An Analytic Simulation

Model of Human Reproduction with Demographic and Biological Components." *Population Studies* 19 (March 1966): 297-310.

Riemer, R., and Whelpton, P. K. "Attitudes toward Restriction of Personal Freedom in Relation to Fertility Planning and Fertility." *Milbank Memorial Fund Quarterly* 33 (January 1955): 63-111.

Ryder, Norman B., and Westoff, Charles. "National Fertility Study." Paper presented to the Notre Dame Conference on Population, December 1966.

Sagi, Philip C.; Potter, Robert G., Jr.; and Westoff, Charles. "Contraceptive Effectiveness as a Function of Desired Family Size." *Population Studies* 15 (March 1962): 291-96.

Schacter, Joseph, and McCarthy, Mary. "Illegitimate Births: U.S. 1938-1957." *Vital Statistics—Special Reports,* vol. 47, no. 8 (September 30, 1960).

Schofield, Michael. *The Sexual Behavior of Young People.* London: Longmans, 1965.

Sheps, Mindel C. "Applications of Probability Models to the Study of Patterns of Human Reproduction." In *Public Health and Population Change,* ed. Sheps and Ridley. Pittsburgh: University of Pittsburgh Press, 1965.

————. "Pregnancy Wastage as a Factor in the Analysis of Fertility Data." *Demography* 1 (1964): 111-18.

Sheps, Mindel C., and Perrin, Edward B. "Changes in Birth Rates as a Function of Contraceptive Effectiveness: Some Applications of a Stochastic Model." *Journal of the American Public Health Association* 53 (July 1963): 1031-64.

Talwar, P. P. "Adolescent Sterility in an Indian Population." *Human Biology* 37 (September 1963): 256-61.

Tietze, Christopher. "Differential Fecundity and the Effectiveness of Contraception." *Eugenics Review* 1 (January 1959): 131-32.

————. "Pregnancy Rates and Birth Rates." *Population Studies* 16 (1961): 31-37.

————, ed. *Bibliography of Fertility Control, 1950-1965.* Publication no. 23, National Committee on Maternal Health, Inc. New York, 1965.

Tietze, Christopher, and Lewit, S. "Patterns of Family Limitation in a Rural Negro Community." *American Sociological Review* 18 (October 1953): 563-64.

United Nations, Department of Social Affairs, Population Division.

*Foetal, Infant and Early Childhood Mortality.* Vol. 1, *The Statistics.* New York: United Nations, 1954.

Vincent, Clark E. "The Unmarried Father and the Mores." *American Sociological Review,* vol. 25, 1960.

_____. *Unmarried Mothers.* Glencoe, Ill.: Free Press, 1961.

_____, ed. "Premarital Sex Relations: The Facts and the Counselor's Role in Relation to the Facts." A symposium in *Readings in Marriage Counseling.* New York: Thomas Y. Crowell, 1957.

Westoff, Charles, *et al. Family Growth in Metropolitan America.* Princeton: Princeton University Press, 1961.

_____. *The Third Child.* Princeton: Princeton University Press, 1963.

Whelpton, Pascal K., and Kiser, C. V., eds. *Social and Psychological Factors Affecting Fertility.* 5 vols., 1943, 1946, 1950, 1952, 1958.

Whelpton, Pascal K.; Campbell, A.; and Patterson, J. *Fertility and Family Planning in the United States.* Princeton: Princeton University Press, 1966.

Young, Leontine. *Out of Wedlock.* New York: McGraw-Hill Book Co., 1954.

Zell, J. R., and Crisp, W. E. "A Psychiatric Evaluation of the Use of Oral Contraceptives: A Study of 250 Private Patients." *Obstetrics and Gynecolgy* 23 (May 1964): 657-61.

# Index

68; leading to dead ends, 67; leading to success in obtaining abortion, 67; number of, 66; percent successful, 69-71; related to total consulted during search, 65-66
Friends: as channels of abortion information, 144; and decision-making process, 54-56; as fresh starts, 66-68; as man involved in pregnancy, 42; older, 54; *See also* Boyfriend; Girl friend

Generational lines, as barriers to the flow of information, 141
German measles. *See* Rubella
Geography, as basis for acquaintance, 127
Girl friend: accompanied woman to abortionist, 95; as channel of abortion information, 144; as fresh start of successful chains, 69, 77; secrecy of abortion from, 114-16; told after abortion, 114
Goals of research, 16
Gossip: about other women's abortions, 130-32; in encouraging deviant behavior, 132-33; and informal social structure, 131; and maintaining conformity, 132; and normalizing abortion, 133; as a source of information on abortion, 11-12
Gossip factor, 134, 137-38
Guesses, educated, 123

Health problems, as reason for abortion, 51
Help, requests for, 138
Home remedies, 45
Homes: private, as places for abortion, 97; for unwed mothers, 151
Hospital abortion. *See* Legal abortion
Hospitalization: following catheter-type abortions, 83; for complications of abortions, 100-101; for hemorrhage owing to self-induced abortion, 80; for incomplete abortion, 85
Hotel rooms, as places of abortion, 97
Household composition, 28
Husband: changes in relationship with, 108; as man involved in pregnancy, 41; and role in decision

making, 51; told of premarital abortion, 109

Identity of informants, disguising, 26
Illegal operation, 73. *See also* D. and C. abortions
Illegitimacy, 150-51; as alternative to abortion, 49-50
Impression of abortionist, 97, 99
Inclusion of persons in description of search, 60
Incomplete abortions. *See* Complications of abortion
Independence of study group, 30
Infection, resulting from abortion. *See* Recovery
Informants: as owners of information, 17; protection of, 17-18, 26. *See also* Abortion specialists; Study group
Information, abortion: channels of, 144-45; network, 9-11; received from others, 130-34; transmitted to others, 134-38
Initiative, for transmission of abortion information, 12
Intercourse: casual, 194; incomplete, 44
Interviewing procedures, 21-24
Invisibility of solutions to unwanted pregnancy, 152

Japan: abortion policy of, 4; as source of legal abortion, 87
Justification of behavior in interviews, 23

Kinship: and acquaintance networks, 124, 128; as barrier to the flow of information, 141. *See also* Relatives

Laboratory, as a source of pregnancy test, 48
Leads, to abortionists, 71-76; number obtained, 72
Legal abortion, 79; access to, 163-64; as an alternative to illegal abortion, 89-90; annual incidence of, in U.S., 5; attitudes of the general population toward, 31-33; attitudes of the study group toward, 31-33; avail-